Reconsidering Radical Feminism

Sexuality Studies Series

This series focuses on original, provocative, scholarly research examining from a range of perspectives the complexity of human sexual practice, identity, community, and desire. Books in the series explore how sexuality interacts with other aspects of society, such as law, education, feminism, racial diversity, the family, policing, sport, government, religion, mass media, medicine, and employment. The series provides a broad public venue for nurturing debate, cultivating talent, and expanding knowledge of human sexual expression, past and present.

Recent volumes in the series include:

A Queer Love Story: The Letters of Jane Rule and Rick Bébout, edited by Marilyn R. Schuster
We Still Demand! Redefining Resistance in Sex and Gender Struggles, edited by Patrizia Gentile, Gary Kinsman, and L. Pauline Rankin
The Nature of Masculinity: Critical Theory, New Materialisms, and Technologies of Embodiment, by Steve Garlick
Making a Scene: Lesbians and Community across Canada, 1964–84, by Liz Millward
Disrupting Queer Inclusion: Canadian Homonationalisms and the Politics of Belonging, edited by OmiSoore H. Dryden and Suzanne Lenon
Fraught Intimacies: Non/Monogamy in the Public Sphere, by Nathan Rambukkana
Religion and Sexuality: Diversity and the Limits of Tolerance, edited by Pamela Dickey Young, Heather Shipley, and Tracy J. Trothen
The Man Who Invented Gender: Engaging the Ideas of John Money, by Terry Goldie
Selling Sex: Experience, Advocacy, and Research on Sex Work in Canada, edited by Emily van der Meulen, Elya M. Durisin, and Victoria Love

For a complete list of the titles in the series, see the UBC Press website, www.ubcpress.ca/sexuality-studies.

Reconsidering Radical Feminism

Affect and the Politics
of Heterosexuality

JESSICA JOY CAMERON

UBCPress · Vancouver · Toronto

© UBC Press 2018

All rights reserved. No part of this publication may be reproduced, stored in a retrieval system, or transmitted, in any form or by any means, without prior written permission of the publisher, or, in Canada, in the case of photocopying or other reprographic copying, a licence from Access Copyright, www.accesscopyright.ca.

27 26 25 24 23 22 21 20 19 18   5 4 3 2 1

Printed in Canada on FSC-certified ancient-forest-free paper (100% post-consumer recycled) that is processed chlorine- and acid-free.

ISBN 978-0-7748-3728-6 (hardcover)
ISBN 978-0-7748-3729-3 (pbk.)
ISBN 978-0-7748-3730-9 (PDF)
ISBN 978-0-7748-3731-6 (EPUB)
ISBN 978-0-7748-3732-3 (mobi)

Cataloguing-in-publication data for this book is available from Library and Archives Canada.

Canada

UBC Press gratefully acknowledges the financial support for our publishing program of the Government of Canada (through the Canada Book Fund), the Canada Council for the Arts, and the British Columbia Arts Council.

This book has been published with the help of a grant from the Canadian Federation for the Humanities and Social Sciences, through the Awards to Scholarly Publications Program, using funds provided by the Social Sciences and Humanities Research Council of Canada.

Printed and bound in Canada by Friesens
Set in Sabon and Myriad by Marquis Interscript
Copy editor: Robert Lewis
Proofreader: Helen Godolphin
Indexer: Christine Jacobs
Cover designer: Sigrid Albert

UBC Press
The University of British Columbia
2029 West Mall
Vancouver, BC V6T 1Z2
www.ubcpress.ca

Contents

Acknowledgments / vii

Introduction: Radical Attachments / 3

1 Radical Deconstructions of Heterosexual Practice: Reading Heterosexual Intercourse / 21

2 Naming Experience, Experiencing a Name: Discourse, Sexual Assault, and the Workings of Affect / 41

3 Heterosexist Pornographies and Sex Work: Transgression, Signification, and the Politics of Shame / 61

4 Paranoid Witness and Reparative Disengagement: Reading Feminist Writings on Heterosexuality / 83

Conclusion: Ambivalent Attachments / 103

Notes / 109

Bibliography / 137

Index / 147

Acknowledgments

This book would not have been possible without the help of many people along the way. A big thank you goes out to Shannon Bell for offering years of guidance and support. I continue to find inspiration in her commitment to throw aside illegitimate expectations. Lorraine Hussey helped provide the vision for this project through our early feminist discussions. Thank you. The politically on-point Allyson Mitchell offered valuable insight early on as did Brenda Cossman, Meg Luxton, and Barbara Crow. Caitlin Fisher, Judith Hawley, Betty Albert, and the AGYU also offered assistance along the way.

I am grateful to Darcy Cullen, Ann Macklem, and the staff at UBC Press for helping me bring this book to fruition. My anonymous reviewers, while sometimes tough, helped me to improve the quality of the manuscript. Thank you.

Heartfelt appreciation goes out to my writing companions Heather McLean and Colleen Bell (a.k.a. Bells). Last but not least, I thank my family. My brother, Kevin, deserves praise for daring to read an earlier draft of the manuscript. My parents, Christine and Bruce, deserve praise for daring to raise me. Thank you. And a special thank you goes out to my weirdo, Jeremy Hunsinger; we need more cats.

Reconsidering Radical Feminism

Introduction
Radical Attachments

I became a feminist at age fourteen. I didn't yet know what such a person was called, but, in retrospect, that's what I was. I spoke out against the differential treatment I received as a girl; I corrected damaging gender stereotypes reproduced by teachers and classmates; I questioned the idea that boys were supposed to fall in love with girls, that girls were supposed to fall in love with boys, and that marriage was the inevitable outcome. As I grew older, I developed more of a language through which to express my thoughts and ideas. I became interested in the notion of patriarchy. Here, I found a way to critique multifaceted systems of oppression that devalued women and compromised female autonomy. But I wanted to learn more. Near the end of high school, I began reading feminist books on summer break. At that time, comprehending the relatively accessible prose of social activist and writer bell hooks was nearly impossible, but I continued on, eventually finding works by radical feminists Andrea Dworkin and Catharine MacKinnon. And so, as it happened, I adopted the label "radical feminist." My particular brand had a couple of defining features: I believed male supremacy was a global, transhistorical phenomenon aimed at the control of female sexuality and that a radical overthrow of the prevailing social order would be necessary to achieve equality. But, of course, things changed again, as they often do. During my undergraduate and master's studies, I was introduced to socialist, sex-positive, and poststructural feminism. Socialist feminism taught me that gender is not the only axis of oppression. Sex-positive feminism enabled me to investigate gendered sexual practices without an obsessive focus on injury. And poststructural feminism provided relief from the political weight of structural analyses of patriarchy's "truth." I was untethered from radical feminism's fury and given opportunities to enjoy theoretical experimentation in my work life and sexual experimentation in my personal life without the constant worry of proper feminist comportment.

I am, of course, not the only feminist who has shifted away from radical feminism. Due in part, no doubt, to the feminist sex wars, many academics and activists have. The heated debates of the feminist sex wars dominated the 1980s and 1990s, creating the impression of a false polarization between feminisms deemed anti-sex and those deemed more sex-positive. Radical feminism, seen as archetypal of the anti-sex camp, was vocal in pointing out the wrongs of sexuality as practised under patriarchal social relations. Heterosexual intercourse was too often an exercise in male hedonism, sexual assault was all-pervasive, and pornography and sex work, as reflections of unequal social relations, served male pleasure no matter the costs to women. Sex-positive feminism, conversely, frequently focused on the wrongs of radical feminism. Here, the concern was erasures of female sexual pleasure through an overemphasis on sexual danger. When patriarchy is seen as an all-encompassing system of male power and control, the agency women do in fact exercise under unequal relations is overlooked. Although many different feminisms were involved in the sex wars, all with varying views of the matters under consideration, the focus crystallized around debates between feminists who thought women needed to be protected from oversexualization on social terms that were never of their own choosing and those who felt women needed to be liberated from social and sexual paternalism. It is my view that sex-positive feminism eventually won the day and that this marked the near unanimous defeat of radical feminism in many activist and academic circles.[1]

Yet my own interest in radical feminism had not been completely extinguished; it reemerged for me while I was pursuing my doctorate. I was fortunate to receive a scholarship that enabled me to make art that complemented my academic work. Focused on performance and video, I made art that dealt with feminist themes pertaining to sexuality. I was, or so I thought, creating sex-positive imagery that adhered to the poststructural understanding that texts have no inherent meaning. But to my disappointment, my work was sometimes interpreted against my intentions. Nonfeminist viewers did not always recognize the intervention I was making in dominant representations of female sexuality and instead read the videos and performances as alternative erotica. I was left to reflect on my work. What I found was a feminist politics different from what I had previously recognized; my work, it appeared, was explicitly addressing patriarchal representations of female sexuality. More specifically, my imagery had what I identified as a radical feminist sensibility. But how could this be the case given my self-confessed sex-positive feminist commitments? It seemed that I was unconsciously expressing an attachment to a radical feminist politics – that I was acting out commitments to an antiquated feminist framework that was already defunct.[2] Or was it? This was the question I was left to explore.

Reconsidering Radical Feminism contends that reducing radical feminism to little more than a flawed moment in feminist history is shortsighted.[3] More specifically, this book revisits the feminist sex wars through the use of queer, poststructural, and affect theory to examine how readers develop passionate attachments to particular feminist theories. Understanding passionate attachments benefits from queer theorist Eve Kosofsky Sedgwick's question of what knowledge "does." This approach is concerned less with the truth of knowledge than with its performative effects and affects. I ask not only how feminist knowledges *do* theoretically and politically but also how they *do* affectively through the theoretical frameworks they employ and the politics they profess. The focus here is on the implications of feminist knowledges. In part, the labour that feminist arguments perform is to position readers as gendered subjects; feminist arguments, we might say, interpellate readers in particular kinds of ways. This focus moves away from a continued concern with the rights and wrongs of seemingly oppositional feminist theories in order to explain how readers become invested in conflicting political and theoretical frameworks.[4] Because passionate attachments are developed through psychoanalytic processes of identification that mirror those at play in subject formation and because subject formation is never complete, I conclude that we develop ambivalent investments in the confused particularities of our feminist existence. Here, we begin to answer the question of how seemingly contradictory political and theoretical feminist frameworks might be emotionally and intellectually attractive.

By using queer, poststructural, and affect theory to revisit the politics of heterosexuality through the legacy of the feminist sex wars, I also maintain the poststructural position that heterosexual practices have no inherent or fixed universal meaning while validating radical feminism's claim that they are often deployed as gendered strategies of stratification. Because queer and poststructural feminisms are interested in unhinging identity from fixed, overdetermined social structures, the focus tends to be on future possibilities opened up by nonheterosexual, nondualistic sexualities and gendered identities. As a result, heterosexuality is often displaced as an object of political and theoretical study. *Reconsidering Radical Feminism* redirects the tools developed by contemporary feminisms to investigate important questions asked by radical feminists of heterosexuality while further disrupting some of the ways that radical feminism has been unfairly characterized.[5] This project is unique in its endeavour to sanction a stigmatized feminist framework – at least when speaking about the writing of Dworkin and MacKinnon – through work that tends to enjoy more academic legitimacy. The project also destabilizes many sex-positive critiques of radical feminism and begins the work of bridging generational divides constructed and reinforced through the feminist sex wars.

Radical Feminism and Its Discontents

My argument that radical feminism still has something to offer to a politics of heterosexuality is perhaps strange given that I propose to use poststructural feminism, along with queer and affect theory, in order to prove it. Exploring the seemingly irreconcilable political and epistemological differences between radical and poststructural feminism can serve to demonstrate the benefits of my project. For starters, radical and poststructural feminism employ different theories of knowledge. Modernist discourses, like radical feminism, tend to rely on conceptions of ideology. Originally a Marxist concept, ideology is defined by philosopher Louis Althusser as "a 'representation' of the imaginary relationship of individuals to their real conditions of existence."[6] In this way, it is a false set of ideas used to conceal unjust material relations in the interests of the ruling class or, in this case, the ruling gender. Ideology is placed in opposition to knowledge, which is equated with freedom, progress, or liberation.[7] When questions of heterosexuality are viewed in terms of ideology, we speak of representations of sexual relations between men and women that obscure the manner in which heterosexuality is practised in ways that privilege male partners. The purpose of critical inquiry, in this schema, is to expose structures, causalities, and truths that underlie ideology so that heterosexuality might be practised more equitably. Poststructural theory, conversely, is interested in narrative and genealogy. Here, the focus becomes the social *implications* of the stories we tell and the ideas we hold rather than fixed structures and truths. The lineage of concepts, institutions, and social practices becomes more important than discovering their cause. It is not surprising, then, that poststructuralists favour discourse over ideology. Discourse does not attempt to discover the truth about concrete material conditions underlying representation since, for discourse, representation *is* what shapes material reality.[8] This is to say that discourse has the *effect* of truth; it exists as the means through which all knowledge is produced, whether it be liberatory *or* in line with the powers of domination. Again, it is not that some discourses are true and thus knowledge and that others are false and thus ideology. Rather, different discourses, including heterosexuality as pleasure and heterosexuality as oppression, compete for the status of truth.

We find further irreconcilable differences between radical and poststructural feminism in their conceptualizations of power. Power, for modernists, is top-down. It is something that is held by the few and used against the many for the purposes of domination. According to this approach, men hold sexual power and exercise it on women. In opposition to the view that power is located within and disseminated from particular institutions and persons with abilities to effect influence, poststructural feminists take their direction from philosopher Michel Foucault's position that power is productive. For Foucault, power does not simply operate as a prohibition against those without it; it is not an external force that acts upon the subject. Power is instead transmitted by and through all subjects regardless of social location.[9] The subject is formed through power or, as queer theorist Judith Butler articulates it, "what 'one' is, one's very formation as a subject, is in some sense dependent upon ... power."[10] Here, there is no distinction to be made between power as "acting on" subjects and power as "acted by" them; power simultaneously produces subjects and their agency.[11] In contrast to radical feminism, poststructural feminists disagree that woman can serve as both the subject and object of sexual liberation.

These differences concerning epistemology and power are tied to irreconcilable approaches to questions of identity. In *Gender Trouble*, Butler explains these differences vis-à-vis the politics of representation: "On the one hand, *representation* serves as the operative term within a political process that seeks to extend visibility and legitimacy to women as political subjects; on the other hand, representation is the normative function of a language which is said either to reveal or to distort what is assumed to be true about the category of women."[12] Radical feminism resides in the first camp; it holds onto the category of "woman" as a means of identifying and correcting political inequities. This is to say that radical feminism is aligned with an identity-politics position in presupposing the category of woman as a site from which to conduct research and forward political demands. Here, feminist analyses of heterosexuality must begin and end with how such practices affect women. Poststructural feminism, conversely, believes that this identity-based strategy continually reinvents woman as an object of misrepresentation.[13] As a result, poststructural feminism takes a post-identity-politics position that remains conscious of how analyses of gender and sexuality can reproduce identity categories according to disadvantageous terms.

These two contradictory views of representation have been hotly debated because they hold important implications. Emphasizing contingency, relationality, and intersectionality enables postidentity or poststructural feminists to investigate the lived implications of social identity without fixing gendered subjects within identity categories they did not themselves choose. In other words, the self-reflexivity of postidentity thinking provides tools to disrupt the naming function of its own theorizing; it provides tools to guard against the manner in which feminism can inadvertently assume and thus reproduce particular kinds of gendered subjects as a by-product of its own thinking. Here, postidentity thinking opens possibilities for new social constructions of gender. Identity-based thinkers, such as radical feminists, might offer the rebuttal that in focusing so heavily on the political implications of gendered codifications, postidentity feminisms lose sight of the socio-economic contexts that have produced these codifications to begin with.[14] Here, beginning with the category of woman is not a problem if doing so helps to disclose gendered violence and encourages social transformation.[15] It is argued that because gender and sex have been used as a strategy of stratification, eliminating this stratification necessitates that it first be identified. In addition, identity-based feminism necessitates the identification not only of patriarchal social relations but also of female subjects as bounded and distinct entities who are separate from men and who can work toward the transformation of sexist practices and institutions to ameliorate their situation. Refusing to do so runs the risk of leaving gendered stratification, along with the social, political, and economic structures that support it, uncontested. For this reason, identity-based thinkers, like radical feminists, sometimes criticize poststructural feminism as a demobilization of feminist thought.

Based on these differences between radical and poststructural feminist theories of knowledge, power, and identity, it seems impossible to hold both positions simultaneously. Likewise, it seems impossible to use one as a methodology for studying the other as an object of analysis. But that is what I intend to do. My intellectual and political commitments to sex-positive feminism, as well as to poststructural feminism, do not dull what I perceive to be the seductiveness of radical feminism despite its shortcomings. Reconciling these theoretical and, more importantly, emotional contradictions is difficult. As a result, this project begins from within this discrepancy, where conflicting political and theoretical frameworks hold intersecting and contradictory intellectual, political, and emotional investments.

The Psychic Life of Feminist Theory

Popular thought assumes that we adopt or reject arguments and frameworks on the basis of their theoretical and political validity alone. I contend that our allegiances are far more complicated, that we develop passionate attachments to feminist theories due in part to how they position readers as gendered subjects. We are able to hold contrary investments in seemingly incompatible feminist frameworks because investments are not rational; they are emotional. The attachments we form to feminist arguments and frameworks can be understood through what Sigmund Freud termed "cathexis" – libidinal investments in persons, places, ideas, and things.[16] Cathexis gestures toward an inherent intimacy between knowledge and the emotional or psychological. As literary critic Shoshana Felman explains, psychoanalysis and learning are always closely intertwined; when we do one, we are necessarily doing the other even if we are unaware that this is the case.[17] When we learn new or relearn old knowledges, we engage in the work of reorganizing our psychic selves, just as the therapeutic process is a means through which we are reoriented toward our understandings of self and the world around us.

When cathexis is examined specifically in relation to questions of academic theory, we see that we develop attachments to theory in response to personal sites of significance and that theory is itself productive of personal significance. Theorist, curator, and artist Natalie Loveless concurs: "the locations that we theorize from are always grounded in what moves us most deeply, in that which we are driven by and to which we are driven."[18] Feminist theorist Robyn Wiegman makes a similar argument when she writes that academic knowledges, particularly those pertaining to questions of identity, are "inseparable from the projections, attachments, and affects that propel them."[19] Indeed, our "objects of study are as fully enmeshed in fantasy, projection, and desire as those that inhabit the more familiar itinerary of intimate life."[20] Theory, Loveless and Wiegman might concur, is constitutive of how we experience the world insofar as theory shapes how we feel within and in relation to the world, and we develop attachments to theory on the basis of how we have experienced the world thus far. As a result, our relationships to theory are often passionate whether they are based on love or hate. Psychoanalytic theorist Deborah Britzman uses the language of theory kindergarten to describe this personification of knowledge wherein knowledge is experienced as "either friend or foe."[21] The problem arises, she continues, when the complexity of this relationship goes unacknowledged. When the psychological significance of theory is not recognized, an important segment of our knowledge remains unthought – an entire realm of relations between affect, ideas, and objects.[22]

Much of the psychic significance of theory is shaped by how texts position us as readers. We accept and reject arguments and frameworks on the basis of how we are interpellated, or brought into social existence, by them. The manner in which the subject is formed in relation to the text can be theorized through Butler's important work *The Psychic Life of Power*. In explicating her theory of gender constitution, she builds on Althusser's idea of the interpellative hail that inaugurates individuals into a "certain order of social existence."[23] She cites his famous example of a police officer's halt of an individual walking down the street. The hail of the individual being apprehended by the law is made concrete through the individual's ability to recognize the hail as addressing him or her according to a particular set of terms. This is to say that the meaning of the hail is confirmed by the individual's response to it. The gendered, raced, and classed subject, like Althusser's criminal, is also produced through an inauguration along particular discursive lines that often preclude the possibility of being inaugurated along others. But the performative call produces us as social agents based on the terms of discursive formations that were already always prior to our social existence; "to persist in one's being means to be given over from the start to social terms that are never fully one's own."[24] Here, we see that the inauguration of the subject is always an epistemic process wherein existence itself is produced through discursive codifications.

Because we are brought into social existence according to terms that precede our being and because there is no space for social existence outside discourse, Butler contends, we develop a dependency on the law that marks our inauguration into sociality. But this inauguration is also the mark of our subjugation. We yield to the law as a kind of "narcissistic attachment" to our existence because we would "rather exist in subordination than not exist."[25] And insofar as theory carries its own interpellative effects, we can think of the attachments we form to theory in a manner similar to how we think of our attachments to law. Feminist theory produces gendered subjects according to those terms made available by the text.[26] But how do we as readers turn toward and develop attachments to different feminisms? We do not simply become particular kinds of feminists through our encounters with particular kinds of feminist texts (although this is no doubt significant). We must first recognize ourselves as being in line with the call to feminism – which often remains unnamed in our early feminist encounters but becomes increasingly discriminatory as we pick up and discard different frameworks of analysis. In other words, becoming a feminist – this kind of feminist and not that – requires that we already recognize ourselves as being in accordance with political, theoretical, and epistemological orientations as they are embodied in texts. When we cannot recognize ourselves as being in line with the text, the text is rejected. This is to say that our acceptance or rejection of feminist texts, frameworks, and arguments has more to do with how we recognize ourselves in and through them than it does with the actual texts, frameworks, and arguments themselves.

This theory concerning the psychic significance of texts vis-à-vis their interpellative effects is further complicated by the workings of affect. Affect has been understood in different ways by different theorists; here, I borrow queer literary scholar Ann Cvetkovich's openness to ambiguity between affect, emotion, and feeling.[27] Affect theorist Sara Ahmed takes a similar tack in writing about emotion as a cultural practice that is active in the constitution of social movements and national identities.[28] This approach lends itself to an argument that emotion is constitutive of attachments to arguments and frameworks of analysis. It is true that intellectual subjectivities come into being through texts, but feminist readers only sometimes turn toward the feminist "name." More often, we turn toward the affective orientation of the arguments and frameworks we encounter.[29] And because "affect can be understood as a dynamic relationship between the text and the reader," as media sex scholar Susanna Paasonen contends, a text's affective significance lies less with the text itself than with the reader's relationship to it.[30]

When affect is understood to be relational, as for Paasonen, and thought is understood to acquire meaning only when steeped in feelings, as argued by psychoanalytic theorist Ruth Stein, we are given a framework through which to view attachments to feminism.[31] Our desiring investments and unconscious identifications affect how we receive texts. In other words, texts acquire meaning, both in content and significance, through the manner in which our psychic attachments shape our affective relations to them. We are the ones who create the affective dependencies to which we turn. But since this process is always mediated in part by the unconscious, our access to the text is further enabled or disenabled in ways that are often outside our conscious control. The very act of being drawn to a particular body of literature for the purposes of meaning making, our reading and writing practices, and our interpretive habits all constitute their own attachments in ways that mean beyond the scope of the theories we are thinking through.[32] The presence of affect as mediating the reader's and writer's interactions with theory indicates, as argued here, that reading and writing are never simply cognitive processes but are always passionate, whether these attachments are positive or negative. Or, as Britzman concludes, "we reside in theory from the inside out ... through a theory of affect."[33]

The Feminist Sex Wars and the Politics of Heterosexuality

Each chapter in *Reconsidering Radical Feminism* investigates the complex relationships readers form to feminist arguments and frameworks of analysis by looking at different heterosexual practices hotly debated during the feminist sex wars. Focused primarily on disagreements between radical and sex-positive feminisms, this book starts from the premise that it is difficult both to draw clear lines between different feminist frameworks and to attribute unified political positions to any particular feminism. Feminist frameworks and the political positions attributed to them are often contested. Although there might be very little overlap between radical and sex-positive feminisms, that is not always so with other feminisms. Some radical and socialist feminisms find significant similarities, as do some sex-positive and poststructural feminisms.[34] Another complication in focusing on debates staged during the feminist sex wars is that I am placed in the position of looking backward. As Wiegman argues, "histories of feminist theory are ... attuned more to the anxious needs of the present than to an exploration of the distinctions that attend academic feminism's complex political and intellectual inheritances."[35] Feminist theorist Sharon Rosenberg similarly argues that public memory, whether it resides in popular culture or within the walls of gender studies programs, transmits "particular versions of the past from the perspective of current socio-political struggles, mobilizing attachments and knowledge that serve specified present-day interests."[36] In this way, I must acknowledge that discussing radical feminism's limitations and continued possibilities is necessarily a compromised endeavour. These hesitances aside, I map out debates as I am best able from my current historical location.

Radical feminists are consistently concerned with the coercive conditions under which heterosexuality is practised and reproduced. The most frequent objects of examination are intercourse, sexual assault, pornography, and sex work, as they are seen to be explicit expressions of the gendered political and economic inequalities produced through and productive of heterosexual practice. Catharine MacKinnon's classic radical feminist text *Feminism, Marxism, Method, and the State*, for example, focuses on how women are positioned in heterosexuality. Echoing Marxist conceptions of class, wherein many work for the economic benefit of a few, she asks whether heterosexuality is organized around a division of labour between those who "fuck" and those who "get fucked."[37] This position is summarized in her now famous phrase "man fucks woman; subject verb object."[38] For MacKinnon, this arrangement arises because heterosexuality and heterosexual practices have been shaped by unequal gender relations. Patriarchy does not simply provide the context within which intercourse is practised but has also been constitutive of intercourse itself. In this way, there is no clearly defined boundary that divides heterosexual sex from violence. Forms of sexual violence, including sexual assault, sexual harassment, incest, pornography, and sex work, become "abuses of sex" for MacKinnon; "they are not the eroticization *of* something else; eroticism *itself* exists in their form."[39] Often working closely with MacKinnon, Andrea Dworkin holds a similar position. For her, heterosexuality has been figured according to terms that render it an act of degradation for women; it is a gendering practice that subordinates female subjects by stigmatizing them as female within a patriarchal context. That is why prohibitions exist against male homosexuality; "as long as sex is full of hostility and expresses both power over and contempt for the other person, it is very important that men not be declassed, stigmatized as female, used similarly."[40] Prohibitions against penetrating men, then, become necessary to the maintenance of male power.

For radical feminists who think in terms of a continuum of heterosexual violence, the politics of heterosexual intercourse are closely connected to the politics of sexual assault. Positioning heterosexual sex on one end of the continuum and full-scale sexual assault on the other, continuum theories are able to account for sexual encounters that defy clear-cut classification; they are able to address how power and violence operate in unethical but seemingly nonviolent sexual encounters. For both MacKinnon and Dworkin, these grey areas emerge from heterosexuality's situatedness within patriarchal social relations. As argued by MacKinnon, assault is part of a compulsory heterosexuality that normalizes and sexualizes coercion and force.[41] For Dworkin, it is closely tied to the institutionalized power men hold over women through religion, law, and the rules of cultural production.[42] But although continuum theories are most common, not all radical feminists take this approach. Anti-rape activist and writer Susan Brownmiller, for instance, distinguishes sharply between sex and sexual assault by characterizing sex as passion and assault as nothing more than gendered domination.[43]

In contrast to radical feminism's views of heterosexual intercourse and sexual assault, sex-positive feminism draws clear divisions between the two. Sex-positive feminists often assert that radical feminism's overemphasis on sexism is sex-negative or anti-sex. Understanding all heterosexual encounters as heavily contextualized, or even determined, by patriarchal social relations overshadows possibilities for pleasure and play. In this way, according to sex-positive feminists, radical feminism provides a continuation of repressive social norms that need to be lifted if women are to achieve full sexual liberation and equality. It is for this reason that, in addition to focusing on affirmative possibilities for heterosexuality, sex-positive feminists lend strong support to BDSM and queer sexual practices.[44]

Clearly identifying a sex-positive position on assault is more difficult.[45] The discussion of contested feminist theorists and frameworks inevitably turns to the common characterization of social critic Camille Paglia as anti-feminist despite her self-identification as sex-positive.[46] Her position on sexual assault makes this tension obvious. She argues that sexual assault is wrong and punishable but criticizes the feminist tendency to include within the category of assault far too many sexual experiences that are better understood as "bad sex." Furthermore, she argues that instead of acting like victimized children, women must take responsibility and learn to properly protect themselves by being careful not to place themselves in positions where they might be forced to have sex against their will.[47] Taking a rather different sex-positive position on sexual assault are the authors in the anthology *Yes Means Yes*.[48] Here, the argument is that rape culture can be dismantled through widespread societal appreciation for female sexual pleasure. They assert that the only way to ensure sex is sex, and not assault, is by celebrating affirmative enthusiastic consent.

Heterosexual intercourse and sexual assault are the focus of Chapters 1 and 2. In Chapter 1, "Radical Deconstructions of Heterosexual Practice," I look at radical feminist theories of heterosexual intercourse. More specifically, I defend Dworkin's reading of penetration through the use of poststructural and queer theory. My argument is that Dworkin's work on the codification of heterosexual intercourse – her point that intercourse is often read as synonymous with violation – is valid. This hidden but pervasive representation of heterosexual practice constitutes actors in damaging ways. The validity of Dworkin's argument, combined with its political importance, raises the question of why she is so frequently dismissed. The reason, I argue, is her text's interpellative effects; Dworkin is rejected on the basis of how her text *Intercourse* positions readers as gendered subjects.[49] I conclude with an attempt to recuperate Dworkin through queer theorists Leo Bersani and Ann Cvetkovich. By looking at butch-femme relations that embrace contradiction, ambiguity, and sexual powerlessness, we find an alternative to heterosexist codings of the relation between "fucker" and "fuckee."

Chapter 2, "Naming Experience, Experiencing a Name," looks at the relationships feminist readers form to continuum and either-or theories of sexual assault. I argue that continuum theories are useful in accounting for ambiguous sexual experiences and for the role that sexual discourses play in complicating thinking/feeling responses to sex and assault. In doing so, however, continuum theories further complicate how readers make sense of and name personal experience. Conversely, clear-cut either-or distinctions serve a useful function in dissociating heterosexuality from injury to affirm female sexual agency. These conceptualizations are attractive because of how they position gendered readers to avoid the naming functions of assault. The problem is that sexual experiences are forced into one of two dichotomous camps through processes of exaggeration or erasure in a way that does not always reflect one's thinking/feeling response to the sexual encounters in question. This chapter also looks at different ways that affect can be incorporated into a theory of sexual assault. Feminists sometimes use affect as though it can provide direct access to political truth. But affect does not serve a clear interpretive function; what one experiences as good the other experiences as bad. Affect does, however, continue to be one of the primary means by which individuals distinguish between sex and assault. That is why I argue for a theory of consensus; in explicitly considering how emotion operates in the politics of sex and assault, consensus performs a kind of affective labour that theories of consent simply cannot.

The differences between radical and sex-positive feminism are particularly apparent in how they approach pornography and sex work. As popularly known, radical feminists take an abolitionist position on these two practices. Pornography is understood to be the product of a capitalist, patriarchal society that subordinates and victimizes women. Dworkin's book *Pornography,* for instance, is dedicated to exposing the hypocrisy of this gendered violence in a supposedly free and equal society. "The private world of sexual dominance that men demand as their right and their freedom," she explains, "is the mirror image of the public world of sadism and atrocity that men consistently and self-righteously deplore."[50] MacKinnon concurs. For her, "sexual objectification," as seen in pornography, "is the primary process of the subjection of women."[51] This damage is only compounded by pornography's power to rewrite a woman's "no" as "yes," thereby reducing her access to meaningful consent.[52] In a more recent article, "Unmasking the Pornography Industry," anti-pornography activist Gail Dines takes a similar radical feminist position. She argues that pornography is a teaching tool for male violence against women. It operates as a how-to manual for objectifying women "as fuck objects" and for normalizing sexualized violence.[53] Like radical feminist Robin Morgan, who takes the position that "pornography is the theory, and rape is the practice," Dines conceptualizes sexual assault as a by-product of misogynistic pornography.[54]

Radical feminists take a similar position on sex work, which they argue is produced by and productive of unequal gender relations. For MacKinnon, sex work is part of an all-pervasive system of gender domination, including battery, harassment, incest, and assault. In positioning women as commodities, sex work, like pornography, makes women into objects.[55] Relatedly, radical feminist Kate Millett argues that "prostitutes are in the business not of selling sex but of self-degradation."[56] In this way, they are forced to support "ideological representations of female inferiority."[57] Abolitionist Sheila Jeffreys directly rails against sex-positive approaches to the issue. She rejects the sex-worker rights movement's use of the terms "sex work" and "client." This vocabulary normalizes sex work and "makes it difficult to conceptualise prostitution as a form of violence, a crime against women."[58] Instead, she uses the word "john" because it is contemptuous. Even better than "john," for Jeffreys, is "prostitution abuser" because the term focuses on violence and is equivalent to "batterer" or "rapist."[59]

Sex-positive feminists, not surprisingly, take a very different approach. They espouse an anti-censorship position on pornography, arguing that it is actually *radical feminism* that violates women's rights to free speech by silencing the pleasures of producing and consuming explicit sexual images.[60] Whereas some sex-positive feminists celebrate pornography as an end in itself, others feel that, when properly deployed, it can function to disrupt gendered binaries and proliferate sexual differences.[61] Sex-positive theorists who have been influenced by poststructural feminism sometimes argue that anti-pornography feminism's understanding of the relationship between sexual representation and social and economic inequality is totalizing and deterministic.[62] Not only is the meaning of the image never singular, but it is also difficult to verify absolute causality between explicit sexual representations, including those deemed sexist, and the status of women.[63] Pornography, rather, exists in a complex, ambiguous relationship to social reality.[64]

The sex-positive position on sex work stresses destigmatization and decriminalization. For some sex-positive feminists, this approach means celebrating sex work as a self-determining labour of pleasure.[65] For others, it means treating sex work as any other occupation mediated by gendered and racialized discourses. As emphasized by the Toronto-based sex-worker organization Maggie's, sex workers are entitled to labour rights, including "the right to form unions or professional associations; the right to work independently, collectively or for a third party; and the right to occupational health and safety."[66] Again, we sometimes find similarities between sex-positive and poststructural feminist positions. In line with performance philosopher Shannon Bell's poststructural argument in *Reading, Writing, and Rewriting the Prostitute Body*, sex-positive feminists occasionally hold that the "flesh-and-blood female body engaged in sexual interaction for payment has no inherent meaning and is signified differently in different cultures or discourses."[67] This is to say that rather than uniformly signifying patriarchal domination, the selling of sexual services can have many different meanings.

Chapter 3, "Heterosexist Pornographies and Sex Work," takes aim at sex-positive feminist theorizations of pornography and sex work to better understand how they operate for readers. I argue that sex-positive feminism's fixation on resisting repression relies on Foucault's repressive hypothesis. In doing so, sex-positive feminism engages in a valuation of transgression that works to create divisions between itself and other feminisms while overlooking the specificity of what comes to be known when conservative social norms are overturned. This chapter also examines how desire in pornography and sex work sometimes contributes to a reification of biological difference. This argument, however, needs to be made with caution insofar as desire arises through fantasy and is only loosely connected to the objects toward which it is directed. Continuing with a discussion of affect, I look at how shame enacts attachments to and detachments from pornographic images and commodified sexual practices, as well as attachments to and detachments from the feminist frameworks we use to understand them.

Chapter 4, "Paranoid Witness and Reparative Disengagement," takes a meta-theoretical approach to the issues discussed in the book thus far. I use poststructural and psychoanalytically inflected affect theory to examine radical and sex-positive feminist reading and writing practices – both their affordances and their theoretical limitations. Although radical feminism does a good job of bearing witness to gendered violence, it tends to fall into Sedgwick's reading of psychoanalyst Melanie Klein's paranoid position. As a result, it runs the risk of inciting trauma in the reader through an overemphasis on gendered difference, an uncomplicated emotional resonance, and a tendency to think in terms of the part-object. Sex-positive feminism, conversely, tends toward manic-reparation. Instead of relating to the object of analysis as a contradictory whole, the focus is on positive affect alone, which aligns the theorist with the part-object. This discussion can be tied to an examination of how paranoid and reparative reading and writing practices relate to feminist narrations of subject formation through the notions of past, present, and future.

The book's Conclusion takes a brief look at the question of ambivalent attachments. I review how we develop theoretical and political attachments to feminist arguments and frameworks of analysis in the same way that we do to the discursive laws that constitute our social existence. But the formation of the subject is never complete; we remain unfixed and contradictory. As a result, the attachments we form to theory are equally incomplete. The ambivalence that this situation entails, however, is not of concern; ambivalent attachments signal a reparative positionality.

Radical Deconstructions of Heterosexual Practice
Reading Heterosexual Intercourse[1]

1

Andrea Dworkin is perhaps most infamous for her writing on heterosexual intercourse. In the seventh chapter of *Intercourse*, "Occupation/Collaboration," she writes,

> A human being has a body that is inviolate; and when it is violated, it is abused. A woman has a body that is penetrated in intercourse: permeable, its corporeal solidness a lie. The discourse of male truth – literature, science, philosophy, pornography – calls that penetration *violation*. This it does with some consistency and some confidence. *Violation* is a synonym for intercourse. At the same time, the penetration is taken to be a use, not an abuse; a normal use; it is appropriate to enter her, to push into ('violate') the boundaries of her body. She is human, of course, but by a standard that does not include physical privacy. She is, in fact, human by a standard that precludes physical privacy, since to keep a man out altogether and for a lifetime is deviant in the extreme, a psychopathology, a repudiation of the way in which she is expected to manifest her humanity.[2]

A coarse reading of Dworkin's analysis can be broken down as follows: violation is abuse, intercourse between men and women has been constituted as violation under patriarchal social relations, intercourse is a normal use of women, so the abuse of women through "intercourse-as-violation" is a normal and seemingly compulsory component of heterosexual relations.

This position on heterosexual intercourse has been rejected by feminists and nonfeminists alike. Whereas casual readers tend to argue that Dworkin is an extremist who does not accurately represent their lived experiences, feminist dismissals tend to be more complex. The argument is often that Dworkin posits heterosexual intercourse as having one fixed meaning, universal in scope and political implication. More specifically, it is argued that Dworkin makes an unequivocal equation between all heterosexual intercourse and sexual assault. Literary scholar Jennifer Wicke, for instance, writes that in "Dworkin's view of male sexuality ... intercourse is, simply, rape."[3] This reading was mirrored by many students in my third-year Critical Heterosexualities course after I assigned the chapter. Relatedly, Dworkin is criticized for her gender and sex essentialism. Although rare, there have been a few nuanced analyses of Dworkin written more recently by feminist academics. Rachel Fernflores defends Dworkin against some of her critics, and Tayna Serisier contends that Dworkin "deserves more serious consideration than she is generally given."[4] For the most part, however, her work is regarded as passé and not worth genuine inquiry within most academic feminist circles. At worst, Dworkin is discounted as a ranting fanatic or irrelevant ideologue who does not contribute to real scholarship.

Given Dworkin's use of emotive language, it is not surprising that she is read in a reductive manner insofar as an inflammatory text often incites an inflammatory response on the part of the reader. Despite the heatedness of this terrain, I argue for the validity of Dworkin's theoretical work on the codification of heterosexual practice. This work is premised on the idea that although heterosexual intercourse has no inherent meaning and is signified differently in different discourses, its constitution as assault through the discourse of intercourse-as-violation (as one of many competing discourses) continues to be an important consideration for feminist theorists of heterosexuality. Using Judith Butler, I demonstrate that the discourse of intercourse-as-violation is productive of gendered actors and should therefore be taken seriously. But if this is the case, why is it that Dworkin is so quickly dismissed? I argue it is on account of the interpellative functions that her text holds for readers. Men and women are discursively positioned as perpetrators and victims in a manner that generally falls outside the scope of most subjects' self-conception. Nonetheless, Dworkin's text performs affective labour when read through Leo Bersani's work on gay male sex. Here, I retain the political validity of Dworkin's position while remaining mindful of its interpellative limitations.

Representing Heterosexual Intercourse in Popular Culture

The argument that Dworkin posits heterosexual intercourse as having one fixed meaning, universal in scope and political implication, is misguided. It is far more productive to think of her work as an identification of a particularly troubling representational strategy, not an essential truth. Dworkin is, in fact, quite explicit that she is investigating the political *meaning* of intercourse. We must first remember that, aside from a couple of historical and theoretical chapters, the entire book is a literature review – what we might even call a discourse analysis. Dworkin reads historical literature and theory to identify how violation has been used as a representational strategy for heterosexual intercourse.[5] She cites Dutch gynecologist Theodore Van De Velde's early sociological marriage manual, *Ideal Marriage,* as an example. He writes that "what both man and woman ... wish to feel in the sexual act, is the essential force of *maleness,* which expresses itself in a sort of violent and absolute *possession* of the woman."[6] In marriage, women do not have a choice, according to Christian thinker William Graham Cole's text *Sex and Love in the Bible*. The wife "accepts the fact that man is the head of the woman and submits to her husband's authority not grudgingly and in fear, but willingly, freely, and in joy."[7] Such are the laws of nature according to Cole and Van De Velde. Looking to the Old Testament, bishop Saint Augustine, and French novelist Marcel Proust, Dworkin finds misogynistic justifications for homophobia. Male homosexuality is inadmissible – an abomination, a sin – because in gay sex men are "used" in a way that ought to be reserved for women. Social laws regulating penetration are necessary, then, according to Dworkin, in order to uphold dichotomies of gender and the essential natures of man and woman. As she explains, "men being fucked like women moves in an opposite direction; so there is a rule against men being fucked like women."[8] But as already alluded to, a woman being used as she is supposed to be used does not engender respect. The male characters in Russian novelist Leo Tolstoy's *The Kreutzer Sonata* locate their repulsion for women in the social meanings attached to sexual intercourse, particularly what it signifies for gender inequality, Dworkin explains. Their disgust centres on woman's lower status as expressed through her position in the sexual act even though she is sexually desired as inferior.

It is not just in the classics where the discourse of intercourse-as-violation finds resonance. It is reproduced in seemingly value-neutral cultural definitions of "penetration," such as that found in *Webster's New World College Dictionary*:

> [Penetration includes] the act, power or an instance of penetrating ... the act or an instance of inserting the penis into the vagina or anus ... the depth to which something penetrates, as a military force into enemy territory ... the extension of the influence of a country over a weaker one by means of commercial investments, loans, diplomatic maneuvers, etc. ... [and] keenness of mind, discernment, insight.[9]

We see, then, that representations of intercourse-as-violation are reproduced, by implication at least, in military discourse, colonial discourse, and discourses of knowledge production. Feminist international relations scholar Cynthia Enloe, for example, has spoken at length about the sexualization of warfare and weaponry. These gendered codifications are further racialized as they work to frame Western military interventions in the "East."[10] In an odd play on biblical discourse, penetration signifies the depth of one's knowledge. Here, we find an alignment with Enlightenment practices wherein the knowing subject stands separate from "his" object of knowledge to know its truth (as a practice of domination). We might ask, then, if the word "penetration" is used to denote military domination, colonial influence, and knowledge as mastery, how can it simultaneously operate as a signifier of democratic sexual play in a context where one gender tends to penetrate another?

For Bersani, this double-sidedness of being penetrated as both a sexual act and a position of subordination was already evident in ancient

Greece. Although homoeroticism was relatively accepted, he argues that prohibitions continued to exist against anal sex between men, specifically against taking on the receptive or "passive" position. Being an insertee was seen as incompatible with citizenship and, therefore, political participation.[11] That is because an "ethical polarity" existed in Greek thought between "self-determination and a helpless indulgence of appetites" wherein the first was associated with the active position in sex (the perpetrator) and the second with the so-called passive position (the penetrated).[12] Self-determination being more valued than indulgence meant that the passive role in sex needed to be rejected. As explained by Bersani, "the moral taboo on 'passive' anal sex in ancient Athens [was] primarily formulated as a kind of hygienics of social power."[13] Being penetrated was to abdicate power; it violated the subject's legal and moral integrity, making those who indulged in this pleasure unsuitable for civic authority.[14] His analysis, here, correlates with Dworkin's reading of vaginal intercourse, its codification of the female subject, and the authority lent to those occupying the position of inserter.

With regard to common cultural products, the discourse of intercourse-as-violation can be found in pornography, including overrepresentations of "barely legal" or "teen" models (given current understandings of statutory assault), descriptions of gang-bang that speak of "violating every hole," negotiating compensation for sexual services followed by refusals to pay, and the classic "no" that eventually becomes a "yes."[15] This discourse is further reproduced through colloquial language as seen in popular uses of the word "fuck" as denoting sexual activity simultaneous with its use as an expletive to emphasize negative statements or situations, the use of "suck my dick" as a pejorative insult between men, as well as the use of phrases such as "having your way with her" to mean sexual intercourse.

The discourse of intercourse-as-violation is even reproduced in young adult popular culture. This occurrence becomes particularly evident when we look at narratives underlying the recent vampire craze. In her *Toronto Metro* column "J Spot," Josey Vogels discusses our cultural preoccupation with vampires. She quotes *True Blood* creator Alan Ball's view that vampires are a metaphor for sex, Bram Stoker's 1877 novel *Dracula* being a "thinly vampire-cloaked metaphor for the repressed and conservative sexual mores of the time."[16] Just as "giving into" Dracula's temptation turned women away from the Victorian ideal, so too does this remain the story today. In novelist Stephenie Meyer's *Twilight* series, Bella knows having sex with Edward "could unleash his blood lust," transforming him from a considerate boyfriend into a predatory monster.[17] Do we not see all too clearly a metaphor for the potentially uncontainable and inherently violent "nature" of male sexuality? This is to say that Vogels misses the mark in titling her article "Vampire Mania: It's All about Sex." A more appropriate title might have been "It's All about Avoiding Sexually Dangerous Masculinity." Here, the latent message is that women need to choose the right vampires, those with control over their unlimited prowess, so as not to get bitten.

Naming Acts, Naming Bodies

It is important to consider Dworkin's position that heterosexual intercourse has been figured as violation not only because this hidden but pervasive discourse is replicated in various cultural products but also because naming social acts is productive of how we name bodies. The discursive nature of her argument does not negate its political necessity and weight. When the discourse of intercourse-as-violation is read through cultural theorist Stuart Hall's argument that discourse and materiality are constitutive of one another, we see that although the discourse of intercourse-as-violation does not determine the material act, it has direct implications for how we experience it. As explained by Hall, "questions of culture are not superstructural to the problems of economic and political change; they are constitutive of them!"[18] In other words, the development and reproduction of discourse is not an immaterial process that exists within the realm of the ideal, thereby avoiding the problems of lived reality. Discourse is, rather, a crucial element *of* lived reality.[19] This is to say that even "false" or "untrue" discourses have real material consequences because discourse shapes material reality not through its ability to correctly identify that which precedes its codification but *because* it has the ability to name material reality, which it then posits as truth.

The discursive meanings attached to social practices are further constitutive of actors. As argued by philosopher Friedrich Nietzsche, "there is no 'Being' behind the deed, its effect and what becomes of it; 'the doer' is invented as an afterthought, – the doing is everything."[20] Similarly, Judith Butler argues that subjects are codified, or identified as particular kinds of doers, based on the deeds they perform. Contrary to popular thought, she argues that social agents are the objects, not the subjects, of constitutive acts. Identity is "instituted through a stylized repetition of acts" – through practices that constitute the appearance of substance in identities *as if* it were fixed.[21] Identity and the body, then, are not innate but are produced through "an embodying *of* possibilities both conditioned and circumscribed by historical convention."[22] Sex acts, too, can be thought of as material practices that codify the bodies performing them into specific genders on the basis of how the practices are themselves understood. The social meanings attributed to sexual activities are transferred to the body of their actors in ways that are often productive of gendered difference. Because we necessarily engage in sexual activity through the use of narrative, often gendered narrative, this transference is difficult to avoid. Like all material practices, heterosexual sex is constitutive of gender in that how we know heterosexual sex deeply affects how we know women and men more generally. These knowledges shut down infinite possibilities for existence by slotting it into a set of finite categories predetermined by available discourse. And in so doing, they shape the lived realities in which subjects are immersed.

This production of gendered social positions through material practice – their production in a manner that lends them the appearance of truth – operates by means of codifying anatomy. This process can be explained by looking again to the work of Hall with regard to fabrications of "race." He argues that although race has no essential existence, it has been discursively "*made* to be true."[23] The physical differences of, for example, skin colour, hair texture, or facial features – as real material phenomena – do not bear inherent meaning themselves but are given meaning through racial discourses that "produce, mark, and fix the infinite differences and diversities of human beings through ... rigid binary coding[s]."[24] Furthermore, Hall contends that power coheres around these symbolic differences and that this coherence influences not only how one is understood but how social and economic goods are distributed in society. Although Butler has different political motivations and implications, she makes a similar argument with regard to the production of gender. Sex is often assumed to be the nature onto which gender as a social phenomenon is grafted. In opposition to this view, Butler argues that "sex, by definition, will be shown to have been gender all along."[25] Sex is not the prediscursive foundation upon which gender is built, nor is gender the causal result of a sexed nature, for Butler. Sex, rather, is always already *gendered*. Like race, the physical differences we understand as the basis for sexual dimorphism are produced as such through being lent meanings that render their production invisible. In this way, gendered and racialized identities become verifiable only when measured against the physical differences they are said to describe.

Both Hall and Butler are useful in making sense of Dworkin's work on gendered anatomy. Dworkin writes,

> She, a human being, is supposed to have a privacy that is absolute; except that she, a woman, has a hole between her legs that men can, must, do enter. This hole, her hole, is synonymous with entry ... She is defined by how she is made ... and intercourse, the act fundamental to existence, has consequences to her being that may be intrinsic, not socially imposed.[26]

This reading, although incendiary, might be viable but only when read through the discourse of intercourse-as-violation. The female hole exists for the other, as wound, as mark of perpetual vulnerability, when gendered discourse is read back onto biology through sexual practice. In other words, "that slit that means entry into her – intercourse – appears to be the key to women's lower human status" because of how heterosexual intercourse has been discursively constituted alongside a cultural tendency to understand sex as prior to social construction.[27] Dworkin's argument that heterosexual intercourse involves pushing in past bodily boundaries used to define the human subject as inviolate – the "thrusting ... persistent invasion" – can now be read as the effect of a discursive formation wherein gendered discourses of sexual difference and the discourse of intercourse-as-violation serve an interdependent role.[28]

We can surmise, then, that it is not just that material activity codifies actors but that the codification of bodies through discourse also shapes how material practice is read. Even when dissimilar bodies participate in similar material practices, both the actor and the activity itself can be interpreted differently on the basis of which body is present. Pregnancy, for example, is read differently on the body of an adult, middle-class, white woman from how it is read on a racialized, working-class woman or teenaged girl. Returning to heterosexual practice, we can see that it is not simply that sex acts determine how bodies become gendered but also that the codification of bodies into discrete sexes and genders works to codify sex acts themselves. Again, heterosexual intercourse contributes to the production of sex and/or gender, but these productions contribute to the political meaning of intercourse, such that our understandings of intercourse become indistinguishable from how we participate in the activity as gendered beings. This process infers a feedback loop: material practice (the deed) is given meaning through the bodies that perform it (the doers), and performers are codified through their association with the material practice in question. Furthermore, the interconstitution of material practice and acting bodies works to couple gendered doers with particular kinds of sexual deeds or with a particular polarity within a deed performed, and the possibility of performing other deeds is either foreclosed or becomes the condition under which the actor's social being is transformed.[29]

Desiring Subjects and Readers
Given the discursive validity of Dworkin's theory regarding cultural framings of intercourse-as-violation, as well as the manner in which these framings shape gendered actors, we are are left wondering why Dworkin is so quickly discarded. One possibility lies in her theory of heterosexual desire. Heterosexual desire, at least as normatively understood, is sometimes complicated for feminist theorists. Insofar as it is heterosexual, it requires narratives of sexual difference; it requires a recognition of sexual difference – a recognition of gendered others with primary and secondary sex characteristics different from one's own. In other words, the desired objects must first be identified as male or female before they can be desired as such.[30] Markers of gendered difference become sites for desire, and heterosexual desire becomes productive of gendered difference by demarcating certain anatomical features as

desirable and imbuing them with cultural significance. We might even argue that heterosexual desire necessarily objectifies through its requirement that the desired object properly adhere to that which constitutes the social meaning of a particular sex and/or gender. Here, desire serves a regulatory function in helping to produce sexed difference in a manner that is often nonthreatening to a continuity of dominant gender codes. This view is very much in keeping with Butler's reading of the heterosexual matrix wherein "'intelligible' genders are those which in some sense institute and maintain relations of coherence and continuity among sex, gender, sexual practice, and desire."[31]

But Dworkin's view of desire is considerably more concerning. As she explains, heterosexual male desire presupposes violent ontological assumptions and eroticized power differentials. "Male desire in reality is a sexual recognition of female as female, fucking the empirical proof that *she is*."[32] For Dworkin, men tend to desire women in a way that solidifies her being as an object to be owned through the fuck. Herein, men constitute their object of desire and their mode of desiring in a manner that lends support to the discourse of intercourse-as-violation. Women, then, do the reverse, according to Dworkin, by desiring subjects who can confer object status upon them; the desire is *to be* an object – one that can be fucked by a subject. Put another way, women replace a desire for the other with a desire to be desired by the other. This is particularly concerning when we think that what Dworkin is identifying here is a desire to be desired within the specificity of one's embodiment as produced through a gendered discourse that, as we have already discussed, is less than favourable. Dworkin meditates on this gendered desire to be desired:

> What does it mean to be the person who needs to have this done to her: who needs to be occupied; who needs to be wanted more than she needs integrity or freedom or equality? If objectification is necessary for intercourse to be possible, what does that mean for the person who needs to be fucked so that she can experience herself as female and who needs to be an object so that she can be fucked?[33]

Here, we find that desire is framed as a practice of domination through codifications of anatomical difference that enable Dworkin to read "that slit that means entry" and occupation as the key to women's gender inequality.[34]

But readers might note serious shortcomings with Dworkin's analysis of desire even if she is correct that desiring practices ought to be politicized. Some might dismiss Dworkin's position on the basis of its scope, arguing that she has greatly overstated her case. It is surely not true that *all* heterosexual men and women desire in the manner she has articulated. Many heterosexual subjects posit intersubjectivity as the foundation for their desire even though their sexual practice may at times involve negotiated power imbalances. Furthermore, many heterosexual female subjects experience a conflict in wanting to be desired but also wanting to avoid being desired according to the discursive terms identified by Dworkin. Still others may experience a conflict in finding these discourses undesirable but still having some need to feel wanted in relation to them.[35] But, as Dworkin might remind us, although the occurrence of men desiring women as objects and women desiring to be an object of desire for the enjoyment of men is not all-pervasive, these practices do enjoy some pervasiveness.

Perhaps a more significant reason for rejecting Dworkin's reading of heterosexual desire is that it imputes false consciousness to women who partake in and enjoy heterosexual relations. This Marxist idea holds that subjugated classes sometimes maintain their own oppression by ascribing to systems of valuation that work against their self-interest. In the case of Dworkin, women play an active role in bringing forth and maintaining their subordination by practising a desire to be desired on questionable discursive terms. Although we see, here, why Dworkin's chapter is titled "Occupation/Collaboration," the political fallout of false consciousness arguments can be damaging. According to a modernist discourse that critiques certain knowledges as ideology and presumes there is a truth that we might gain access to through correct knowledge, subjects are divided into those who have "good" or "true" knowledge and those who have been duped into holding "bad" or "false" knowledge (thus negating its status as knowledge). But, of course, we never regard ourselves as having been fooled. As philosopher Slavoj Žižek argues, ideological positions are always what we impute to others.[36] In assuming a certain level of ignorance in others, then, false consciousness arguments are condescending and infantilizing.

Here, we arrive at what I believe to be the main reason Dworkin is often thrown out, bathwater and all. My argument is that she is rejected not only on the basis of her negative framing of heterosexual desire (and intercourse) but also on account of how her framing of heterosexual desire can be read to interpellate gendered readers. Whereas subjects with exclusive same-sex object choice are able to dismiss the call as addressing another, readers who enjoy opposite-sex eroticism may find themselves stuck within a limiting range of options. Heterosexual male readers are brought into social being as more than just perpetrators of sexual violence; men can also become desiring subjects who *require* the sexual and social degradation of women. Heterosexual female readers face a different set of interpellative possibilities. Those who reject heterosexuality as configured by Dworkin under patriarchal social relations easily lay claim to the identity of feminist, with those who have survived the perils of heterosexual desire becoming morally superior victims. Readers who accept or, worse, enjoy the play of feminized heterosexual desire become, instead, "nonfeminists" or "wrong-feminists" working at cross-purposes with "real" feminists. This is not to say that women who enjoy heterosexual desire cannot also be feminists who share Dworkin's concerns regarding its performance and reception. It is to say, however, that this last interpellative possibility remains particularly distasteful in telling some heterosexual feminist readers that they are really not feminist at all. Insofar as one of feminism's central aims is to rearticulate how gendered subjects are socially understood, it is rightfully held that our theorizing needs to reproduce gendered subjects, specifically women, as active social agents capable of making informed, self-affirming decisions. Dworkin's work on heterosexual desire falls short.

Gendered Bodies and the Pleasures of Powerlessness

Because Dworkin is sometimes interpreted as presenting a false consciousness argument, it is perhaps surprising that readers turn toward her text at all. I argue that, in addition to lending voice to popular representations of heterosexual intercourse, Dworkin's text *Intercourse* continues to attract readers on account of the affective labour that it performs. Some women attest to experiencing heterosexual intercourse as inherently more risky for them than their male partners. Beyond pregnancy and sexually transmitted infections, the argument sometimes goes, differential vulnerability arises on account of being entered – being touched internally is seen as more significant than being touched on the outside of the body. Dworkin's text bears witness to this perceived reality. But how can we bear witness to experiential differences that arise from the body without returning to essentialist discourses, either those concerning the meaning of anatomical difference or those concerning anatomical difference engaged in heterosexual intercourse? Further, how can we validate the lived experiences of some members of a social group without attributing those lived experiences to characteristics used to construct the social group in the first place? Bersani's queer reading of sex and sexuality provides a framework for moving forward.

For Bersani, sex is a uniquely shattering experience. He makes this argument by drawing on Sigmund Freud's work in "Three Essays on the Theory of Sexuality." For Freud, Bersani contends, "sexual pleasure occurs whenever a certain threshold of intensity is reached, when the organization of the self is momentarily disturbed by sensations or affective processes somehow 'beyond' those connected with psychic organization."[37] This experience is described as a "*jouissance* of exploded limits," as a kind of "ecstatic suffering."[38] Like Freud's contention that pleasure and pain are closely coupled in sexuality, Bersani maintains that sexuality bears an inherent relationship to masochism. This relationship is the result of an "evolutionary conquest" that enables infants not only to survive but also to find pleasure in being overcome by stimuli "for which they have not yet developed defensive ... ego structures."[39] It is this shattering that gives sexuality, according to Bersani, its antisocial character in that the very psychic structures that enable us to establish relations with others momentarily (at least) fall apart.

Ann Cvetkovich makes a similar argument. She draws on Bersani to theorize affective investments in touch as healing but also potentially traumatic. Trauma is represented as a wound or shock wherein the psyche has experienced some kind of violent shattering. This representation can be seen in discourses of sexuality; both trauma and sexuality "invoke the powerful fears of vulnerability that ... being touched can arouse."[40] Cvetkovich explains that being touched emotionally is similar to being traumatized because it often feels physical even if it is primarily a psychic state. In this way, trauma is "equivalent to invasive physical contact" – to being touched on the *inside* or, in other words, a *penetration* after which the ego can never be the same.[41] Here, we begin to see the relation that sex, as psychic shattering, bears to gendered anatomy. The psychic shattering that sex invokes has two modalities according to Bersani: hyperbolic sense of self and loss of consciousness of self. But, as he explains, self-hyperbole is really only a repression of self-abolition. Hyperbole "inaccurately replicates self-shattering as self-swelling, as psychic tumescence" – a psychic tumescence that, perhaps not surprisingly, is mirrored in male anatomy and a "phallicizing of the ego."[42] Female anatomy, conversely, is associated with being touched internally and, therefore, facilitates self-abdication.[43] This is not to say that both "sexes" do not engage in hyperbole, just that men are more likely to manifest self-shattering as its opposite: self-inflation and a defensive solidification of the ego. "It is the [male] self that swells with excitement at the idea of being on top, the self that makes of the inevitable play of thrusts and relinquishments in sex an argument for the natural authority of one sex over the other."[44]

The fact that heterosexual intercourse, as invasive physical contact or penetrative shattering, does not operationalize as an *association* of self-hyperbole and self-abdication with gendered anatomy but is, rather, experienced by some as an *outgrowth* of gendered anatomy finds resonance in Butler's explanation of how sexual difference is formed. If we understand gender as performative, "how precisely are we to understand the ritualized repetition by which such norms produce and stabilize ... the materiality of sex?"[45] In a shift from the language of social construction, and its positing of a material realm that exists prior to signification, Butler speaks of *materialization* wherein the line between the constructed and nonconstructed is understood to be a construction of its own. Sex can be read as the "construction of construction"; matter (in this case, sex) is constructed in a manner that stabilizes its appearance as nonconstructed over time.[46] When sex is understood as a process of materialization, one can pay heed to the materiality of bodies engaged in sexual practices (through a reading of sex as already always gender) without participating in what Butler regards as a desubstantiation of sex or a depoliticization of sexual difference. In this way, feelings of risk stemming from the body as it exists "prior to signification" can be understood as an outgrowth of how matter is solidified through social practice and correlating gendered discourses over time. Both a hyperbolic sense of self and a lost consciousness of self, as tied to the engorged body of one occupying the internal space of another, might feel inherent but that is simply because sex is materialized in popular discourse as having a concrete existence that precedes gender. Here, as Butler contends, sex still *matters* even though "there is no reference to a pure body which is not at the same time a further formation of that body."[47]

Dworkin's *Intercourse* is a text that bears witness to the fact that sex still matters. This act of witnessing is part of the affective labour her text performs. Although affective labour is often associated with neoliberal discipline – the unquantifiable immaterial labours we are increasingly asked to perform without remuneration – affective labour can also exist outside the logic of capital. In the case of Dworkin, this labour takes the form of understanding how sexuality and ideology are mutually informed. Bersani's position that sexual practices are psychically inhabited also speaks to the complicated relations that exist between sexuality and ideology. He argues that sexual inequities do not exist outside the realm of ideology but also that sexual inequities are not solely displaced social inequities; sexual pleasure actually has the capacity to *generate* politics.[48] It is the pleasurable shattering of the self through sex (in relation to gendered fantasies of the body) that enables sexuality to be so easily associated with power and powerlessness, he explains.[49] Here, the fantasmatic movements of the body through sex, gender, and sexuality inform ideological mappings. Although it is important to avoid reifying associations of dominance and submission with gendered dualism, Dworkin might agree with Bersani that we cannot sanitize and sublimate the penis into the phallus by simply conceiving sexuality to be "belatedly contaminated by power from elsewhere."[50]

If gendered ideologies emerge from fantasies of gendered bodies engaged in sexual practice, one strategy of resistance is to resignify the play of power and powerlessness from which we cannot escape. Indeed, for Bersani, phallocentric dissociations of powerlessness are both a defence mechanism and a disavowal of powerlessness's value. Phallocentrism is not simply a "denial of power to women" but also "above all the denial of the *value* of powerlessness in both men and women."[51] Cvetkovich provides a queer rereading of powerlessness by contending that femme sexuality embraces losing control; it is unapologetic in expressing an active and eager desire to get fucked. Femme sexuality does not equate receptivity with passivity, nor does it necessitate the ruse of gendered domination to obscure the joys of temporary fragmentation. In this way, "femme discourses of sexuality depathologize the relation between trauma and sexuality" while acknowledging their interconnectedness.[52] There is an understanding that being touched internally can be both physically and psychically disruptive *and* affirming. Here, radical disintegrations of self are embraced outside reifications of sexual difference.

When read in this way, butch-femme relations provide a powerful alternative to readings of heterosexuality that channel powerlessness and the loss of control inherent to sex into (male) self-inflation and (female) abdication. Put another way, butch-femme relations open space to rewrite the gendered relations that often exist between the heterosexual "fucker" and "fuckee." But this situation does not apply only to female or feminized subjects. The desire to be desired by an other who can fuck the self might still be a scary proposition but one similarly so for heterosexual men. Heterosexual men might not enjoy (or admit to enjoying) the pleasures of being internally physically fucked as often as homosexual and queer women and men, but they can enjoy being internally psychically fucked just the same. If being female, in the words of Dworkin, is synonymous with entry, including a desire for entry, one can interpret this framing in ways that honour the politically generative character of sexuality while destabilizing antiquated heterosexual norms. But

Cvetkovich bids we proceed with caution. This queer desire for getting fucked, she argues, is different from heterosexual acts of penetration that often position the bottom as little more than a humiliated object for the top's pleasure. "So impoverished is the language of sexual power, especially the *loss* of sexual power, that [often] this can only be translated into an active/passive dichotomy, where passivity is always stigmatized."[53] Here, we see that although the meanings attributed to heterosexual penetration are malleable and subject to change, they may still longingly cling to bodies and practices in damaging ways.[54]

Conclusion

After looking at Dworkin's analysis of the discourse of intercourse-as-violation through both poststructural and queer psychoanalytic theory, it would appear that wholesale dismissals of her work have little merit. Understandings of intercourse as associated with vulnerability or humiliation do not have to be inherent truths, fused to gendered bodies, in order to have real-world implications. The discourses we use to understand sexual practice and practices of desire have constitutive effects on social actors through the manner in which actors are situated vis-à-vis the practices in question. In other words, "doers" are produced through practices of doing – practices that are codified in line with how the actors involved have themselves been named. Here, we find that Dworkin's claims that men desire fucking women as objects, that women desire being fucked as objects, that female anatomy is synonymous with entry, and that intercourse might be a mark of women's lower human status are still worthy of political inquiry. Discursive terms are just as important as those that are socio-economic if we are to move toward substantive equality and open space for men and women to fuck as equals. Furthermore, popular criticisms of Dworkin's *Intercourse* – that she is essentialist and anti-sex and that she posits all heterosexual intercourse as rape – become less tenable particularly when we agree she is identifying a "discourse of male truth," not truth itself.[55]

Dworkin herself takes up criticisms levied against her work. She argues that common misreadings of her work are based on the very gendered ideologies she is trying to refute:

> If one's sexual experience has always and without exception been based on dominance – not only overt acts but also metaphysical and ontological assumptions – how can one read this book [*Intercourse*]? The end of male dominance would mean – in the understanding of such a man [or woman] – the end of sex. If one has eroticized a differential in power that allows for force as a natural and inevitable part of intercourse, how could one understand that this book does not say that all men are rapists or that all intercourse is rape? Equality in the realm of sex is an antisexual idea if sex requires domination in order to register as sensation.[56]

Here, we clearly see that according to Dworkin's own perception, she is not anti-sex but anti-sexism. She does not argue that all heterosexual intercourse is rape but rather that codings of heterosexual intercourse as violation, when pushed to their logical conclusion, reveal that sex is often figured *as if* it were rape. Put another way, the material act of intercourse, although often framed through the discourse of intercourse-as-violation, cannot *be* violation if we simultaneously understand that it is ascribed meaning through its functioning in discourse. Dworkin's rebuttal further refutes claims that she is essentialist insofar as arguments concerning the *naturalization* of male dominance and female submission necessarily presuppose that they are not themselves natural.

The only conclusion I am able to draw is that Dworkin can no longer be easily dismissed on account of her totalizing argumentation and that her position on heterosexual intercourse is important. Nonetheless, she continues to be discarded. That is partly due to the fact that she makes what seems to be a false consciousness argument, but there are other reasons for her frequent dismissal as well. Reductive readings enable Dworkin to serve as a straw-person not just for gender conservatives but also for the feminist third wave – a place where poststructural and sex-positive feminists can hang their critiques of radical feminism. We might find that Dworkin is misinterpreted so that she *can* be easily opposed. Sweeping dismissals enable the reader to overlook political questions regarding the status of heterosexual intercourse – how it has been discursively configured and how this discursive configuration lends meaning to its practice in a manner that has constitutive effects.

But it is not simply that misreadings silence what is otherwise an important feminist intervention. As argued by Foucault, discussions of sex and sexual politics strike a deep chord because sexuality plays a central role in how the contemporary subject conceives of the self.[57] Here, I am speaking not only about the manner in which subjects invested in heterosexual intercourse may want to avoid analyzing the negative implications of their sexual practices but also, more importantly, about how subjects come into social being through discourses of heterosexual intercourse. Subjects internalize and form attachments to the social practices they perform in their becomings before the law. When these social practices are situated within discourses that are antithetical to the subject's self-conception, one must reject either the practice or the discursive framing in question. Here, we find that our rejections of Dworkin may be more personal than previously thought; they are motivated by how we perceive ourselves to be positioned in relation to her text. But accepting Dworkin, for heterosexual readers, does not only require a reconsideration of the meanings associated with one's sexual practice; it could also demand a rearticulation of one's theoretical identity and identifications. It makes sense, then, that we adhere to theories that reflect our own self-perception as sexual and intellectual beings – that we attach ourselves, sometimes exclusively, to frameworks that interpellate us in a desired manner.

In addition to interpellating readers as sexual and intellectual subjects, feminist texts also bring us into social being as feeling or emotional beings. Here, we find another reason that readers turn away from Dworkin: her writing style is often deliberately inflammatory. The intention, no doubt, is to elicit an emotional response on the part of readers in order to incite them to action. In practice, however, Dworkin's prose leaves readers, particularly feminist academics, disengaged. It may even be that the affective intensity of her work results in rejections that are largely reactive in character – rejections that operate more as a defence mechanism than as products of contemplative thought. We refuse to be brought into life as thinking/feeling subjects according to the narrow theoretical, political, and affective terms provided by Dworkin's *Intercourse*. It is this refusal, I argue, that closes down the potential for more generous interpretations of her work. Our misinterpretations, when thought of in this way, arise from desiring investments to feel and know heterosexual intercourse and gendered modes of being differently from how they are felt and known through Dworkin. This is particularly the case when we consider that our thinking responses to theory are always already embedded in feeling.

Naming Experience, Experiencing a Name
Discourse, Sexual Assault, and the Workings of Affect

2

In her text *Rethinking Rape*, feminist philosopher Ann J. Cahill outlines two major conceptualizations of sexual assault that have permeated feminist theory. The first sees assault as a crime that is clearly delineated as separate from sex, and the second reads assault along a continuum of heterosexual violence. Unlike other areas of heterosexual politics, neither position is distinctly aligned with radical or sex-positive feminism. Susan Brownmiller, for instance, is a radical feminist who resides in the either-or camp. She argues that assault is a crime of power, as opposed to a crime of sex; perpetrators are not overwhelmed by passion but commit acts of *gendered violence*. Here, the motivation for assault is political domination and social degradation.[1] This conceptualization was important, when it emerged in the 1970s, for opposing sexist assumptions that women are partially responsible for attacks against them by inciting men through their desirability, Cahill explains. The second radical feminist position, popularized by Catharine MacKinnon and Andrea Dworkin, draws links between compulsory heterosexuality and sexual assault. Here, the argument is that assault comes to appear as a normal (albeit extreme) part of heterosexuality's continuum of sexual violence. The lines between sex and assault become blurred through patriarchal social conditions that tie political and economic inequalities to inequalities within the sexual sphere. But, as MacKinnon argues, heterosexual sex within the logic of patriarchy is itself suspect. "Rape is not less sexual for being violent"; "to the extent that coercion has become integral to male sexuality, rape may even be sexual to the degree that, and because, it is violent."[2] In other words, violence, according to continuum theories, is integral to heterosexuality under patriarchal social conditions, with gendered violence becoming eroticized.

Here, I explore some of the strengths and weaknesses of these two frameworks by theorizing the workings of emotion. I am particularly interested in what the relationship between thought and feeling might tell us about the politics of sexual assault. For many thinkers, this relationship is a complex one. Psychoanalytic theorist Ruth Stein, for instance, argues that "our thoughts are steeped in feelings and have meaning for us only if they are accompanied by feelings."[3] Here, it is feeling that lends meaning to thought, without which thought could not be of personal significance. For queer and postcolonial theorist Sara Ahmed, the relationship between thought and feeling is also bodily. Emotions are neither rooted inside the subject to disperse outward nor an imposition on the subject from the outside; emotions are, rather, generated in *contact* with objects.[4] It is in this contact, Ahmed argues, that emotions take on their bodily character and that thinking makes its connection to physical sensation. More than simply evoking a correlative feeling, thinking is made possible through emotion and sensation, and, simultaneously, we cannot feel in the body or psyche in the absence of thought. Ahmed uses the word "impression" to signal this coexistence of bodily sensation, emotion, and thought. Objects make emotional impressions, they impress upon our thinking, and they are capable of making impressions in flesh.[5] Theory also leaves its impressions. Just as practices of assault affect our emotions, thoughts, and bodies, so too do the feminist frameworks we use to understand them.

We might assume that the interrelationship between thought and feeling produces consistent interpretations of bodily experience or that bodily experience, thought, and feeling always clearly align. When it comes to experiences of sexual assault, this is not always the case. It is possible to have sexual encounters that do not *feel* like assault even though we *think* they are and, conversely, to have encounters that *feel* like assault even though, to the best of our analytic abilities, we do not *think* they are. And there are, of course, many situations that leave us not knowing what to think or feel. I approach these ambiguities and ambivalences by examining how personal experience is mediated by both social discourse and feminist theory. Hearkening back to my discussion of the discourse of intercourse-as-violation, we see how thinking/feeling responses to sex and assault are complicated by the "sensational" discursive contexts within which they occur. In turn, our thinking/feeling responses to feminist theories of sexual assault are complicated by the manner in which texts position us as gendered readers. But since thinking occurs only in close concert with feeling, emotion has a complicated relationship to interpretations of sexual experience. I theorize the interpretive function emotion holds for individuals and conclude by looking at how close attention to the workings of affect can shift the way feminists think about the distinction between sex and assault.

Continuum Theories of Sexual Assault (Naming Experience)
Continuum theories of sexual assault do a good job of accounting for sexual experiences that belie clear-cut categorization – experiences that do not neatly fall into the legal categories of assault or consensual sex. Sexual assault proper is often defined as the use of physical force, the threat of physical force, or the deliberate use of intoxicants. But as psychologist and Foucauldian feminist Nicola Gavey explains, just because an experience of heterosexual sex does not clearly adhere to these definitions does not make it ethical or fair. There are plenty of exploitative instances that one might not call assault but that cannot be considered "just sex" either.[6] For Gavey, these might include situations where a man applies pressure but not enough to be considered actual or threatened physical force, where he is excessively rough without proper negotiation, where a women lets sex happen out of a sense of duty or does not feel it is her right to refuse, or where she "allows sex to happen" because she is fearful he will proceed anyway. I would add to this list situations where sexist language is used to describe acts or identity positions without proper negotiation, where emotional manipulation is used to procure consent, and, similarly, where sex is consented to under the pretext of a contract – emotional, financial, or otherwise – to which one party has no intention of adhering. Furthermore, just as

we know certain desires and sexual practices are foreclosed at the level of discourse, so too might that be true of certain "no's." Here, I am thinking about "no" to a particular sex act that seems tightly coupled with another for which the answer is "yes." Another instance is "yes" to a particular sex act but "no" to its common discursive representation. Even more convoluted is "yes" to a particular sex act, "no" to its common discursive representation, but "yes" to that same representation when it is recognized as such by all parties involved.[7] By positioning sexual assault at the far end of a continuum of heterosexual violence, continuum theories are able to account for these kinds of ambiguous sexual experiences.

Continuum theories of sexual assault are also able to account for the manner in which patriarchal discourse can blur the lines between sex and assault. Gavey draws on feminist psychologist Wendy Hollway to outline three damaging discourses that structure heterosexuality: "a male sexual drive discourse, a have/hold discourse, and a permissive sex discourse."[8] The first discourse identified by Hollway normalizes the idea that healthy men experience an overwhelming desire or "need" to have sex. According to the second discourse, women treat sexuality as a means to procure love and children, and, compared with men, they are relatively asexual. The sexual drive and have/hold discourses work together to create unreciprocal relations wherein women are positioned in the role of receiving or rejecting men's sexual advances instead of forwarding their own desires, Gavey explains. Because neither discourse places female desire and pleasure at the forefront of heterosexual sex, their absence can potentially "go unquestioned and unnoticed."[9] The combination of these two discourses also produces men and women as having differential investments in heterosexual relationships. Although no two people will ever want or need the exact same thing from a union, an investment in love or family tends to bear more emotional risk than one predicated on sex. When these two discourses cooperate with the third identified by Hollway, the popularization of permissive sex in the 1960s, we find that it is the liberation of *male* sexuality that becomes celebrated.[10] Summarily, the convergence of these three discourses provides "ample room for ... *un*just sex to take place."[11]

This blurring of the lines between consent and nonconsent at the level of discourse is perhaps most apparent when revisiting Dworkin's identification of how heterosexual intercourse is often framed as violation. The discourse of intercourse-as-violation normalizes heterosexual intercourse not only as an act done to women but also as one that solidifies her subordination. Here, the lines between consent and nonconsent are blurred because consensual sex is conceptualized as nonconsensual. According to this patriarchal framing, either all heterosexual sex becomes nonconsensual, in that consensual sex is foreclosed since heterosexual intercourse constitutes violation and violation is abuse, or all heterosexual intercourse becomes consensual, in that nonconsensual sex is a moot point since heterosexual intercourse constitutes a normal use/abuse of women anyway. Although assault, no doubt, plays a role in shaping conceptualizations of heterosexual sex, I am more interested here in the role that heterosexual sex, when figured through patriarchal discourse, plays in shaping assault. The issue becomes how heterosexual sex needs to be conceptualized in order to operate as a tool for assault. It might be that representations of "normal" heterosexuality are what constitute women as subject to violation in the first place. Or, as Gavey argues, "everyday taken-for-granted normative forms of heterosexuality work as a cultural scaffolding for rape."[12] In this way, the discourse of intercourse-as-violation can be said to provide structural support for sexual assault.

It is not difficult to imagine that this interconstitution of sex and assault at the level of discourse has an effect on how individuals relate to and experience heterosexual sexual encounters; the theories we use to understand heterosexual sex and sexual violence affect lived experience. Continuum theories do a good job of accounting for experiential and discursive ambiguities because they contextualize assault *within* the institution of heterosexuality as it has been historically practised. But in doing so, they can situate assault "not as an exception to, but merely a variation on, normal heterosexual activity."[13] When the sexuality in assault is reduced to violence in sexuality, Cahill notes, it becomes difficult to distinguish between differences in kind – between sexual assault and consensual heterosexual sex.[14] Because continuum theories do not fully acknowledge this fact, because they actually contribute to the discursive ambiguities we have been discussing, continuum theories can heighten the difficulties some subjects have naming experience. Ambiguities at the level of discourse, including feminist discourse, obscure and complicate our personal interpretations. Some might overlook instances of assault or refuse to think about them insofar as the discourse of intercourse-as-violation and continuum theories of heterosexual violence normalize a certain level of exploitation as inherent to heterosexual sex. Others could feel violated in instances that clearly sidestep any legal definition of assault and that involve no perceivable coercion in that feminist discourse has proven all sex to be suspect anyway.[15]

These difficulties that subjects experience naming sexual encounters have an affective dimension. For Ahmed, "the object of feeling," here taken to be heterosexual sex, "both shapes and is shaped by emotion."[16] This is to say that the subject never has direct, unmediated access to sexual experience. Sexual encounters do not stand before subjects as objects to be analyzed from the outside but are shaped by emotions intimately connected to past experience both felt in the body and conceptualized in thought. "How the object impresses (upon) us," Ahmed clarifies, "may depend on histories that remain alive insofar as they have already left their impressions."[17] This provides insight into how heterosexual encounters involving even minimal coercion might be interpreted as full-scale assault. The presence of previously experienced affect and conceptualizations of assault as tied to one's feelings about the practice form both what and how we think. Also explained are many of the unethical sexual scenarios described by Gavey that do not fit the legal definition of assault but that cannot be described as just sex either. Here, women's participation or lack of concern in these vague practices can be understood as tied to previous encounters that were just fine or seemingly "normal." Both scenarios, reading consent as assault and assault as consent, can be explained through Ahmed. As she writes, the object of feeling "may stand in for other objects or may be proximate to other objects."[18] It is the discursive proximity of heterosexual sex to assault, as seen in continuum theories, that can result in experiences of heterosexual sex being read as assault and vice versa. But regardless of whether sexual violence is inadvertently effaced or amplified, we find that the complicated complementary and contradictory relationships between bodily sensation, emotion, and thought, as mediated by discourse, often contribute to difficulties in naming experience.

Either-Or Theories of Sexual Assault (Experiencing a Name)

Positioning Camille Paglia as a sex-positive feminist, or perhaps as a feminist at all, is rather contentious. Here, my use of her work stems both from her self-identification as a sex-positive feminist and from the counterpoint she provides to the continuum theories just discussed. Paglia does not efface experiential differences between heterosexual sex and assault because she theorizes them through an either-or framework. She does so, however, by declaring that date rape does not exist. Feminists, according to Paglia, should stop denying that there are sexual differences based on biology. Male sexuality is inherently uncontrollable in the face of women who "have what they want," and men who have not been properly acculturated will stop at little to get it.[19] Women, Paglia continues, need to recognize this situation and accept that danger is the flipside of the freedom they have fought so hard to acquire. If a woman is out on a date, gets too drunk, or goes to a man's house alone at night and is forced to have sex against her will, it is not rape – it is "bad sex."[20] This is not to say that Paglia condones sexual assault. She understands that it is wrong and that there are clear instances when self-protection is difficult, if not impossible. It is just that, for Paglia, assault proper occurs through archetypes analogous to those of the stranger who attacks from the bushes. Feminists who are unable to distinguish assault from college girls' poor decision making operate on the naive assumption that men can be trusted not to commit sexual assault. Instead, Paglia suggests that women stop playing the victim, stop buying into infantilizing feminist theories, and start taking responsibility for their own self-protection.[21] When things do not go as planned, women should dust themselves off and ensure they do not misread the signs or make bad choices again in the future. Crying rape is not an option.

This kind of either-or division between sex and sexual assault has obvious shortcomings. In addition to an anti-feminist orientation toward blaming the victim, at least in the case of Paglia, it creates too sharp a distinction between sex and assault. As argued by Cahill, "assum[ing] that the realms of sexuality and politics are easily demarcated and separable is to ignore that the violence of rape is peculiarly sexual, that the sexuality on which the phenomenon of rape feeds is peculiarly violent, and that the complex relationship between the two cannot be reduced to one factor."[22] Put another way, assault's status as an act of gendered violence does not make it less sexual. What is specific to sexual assault, what differentiates it from other forms of violence, is its sexual character; sexual assault implicates the sexuality of both assailant and the victim.[23] Paglia does acknowledge that sexual assault is sexualized violence, but, for her, that is not the rapist's intention. He simply wants to get laid. Although a woman may experience forced sex as violent, she is able to claim violence, according to Paglia's logic, only in the most extreme cases – those where she cannot be perceived to have even the smallest amount of culpability. For Cahill and myself, this division between sexuality and violence, wherein the same person cannot simultaneously experience both in a variety of forced sex scenarios, constitutes a misreading of sexual assault's performance and reception.

But Paglia's either-or position on sex and assault also has its benefits. By erasing date rape as an experiential possibility, her theory holds positive implications for the production of female gendered subjects. Simply put, Paglia interpellates women in a favourable manner. Whereas men are universally positioned as potential perpetrators of sexual violence (some of whom may be better acculturated than others), women are divided into two groups: "good" and "bad" self-protectors. By dividing women in this way, Paglia simultaneously produces *all* women as capable of self-protection – as always already possessing the skills needed to stave off the most pervasive forms of sexual assault. Paglia's work, as a result, can be read as empowering through its assumption that women can and *do* protect themselves. Instead of holding sexism or patriarchal myths regarding women's sexuality accountable, instead of waiting for political transformations to bring forth an end to assault, Paglia puts the onus on women themselves, today.[24] Her work stands in the face of the constraints women are often thought to experience within compulsory heterosexuality and, as a result, provides a radical rewriting of gendered agency. This is not to say, however, that the category of date rape is not valuable in politicizing a type of (primarily) heterosexual encounter, only that, in doing so, it runs the risk of reproducing women as subject to sexual violence; politicizing date rape puts it back into public discourse as something that can be done to subjects who are gendered in particular kinds of ways.[25]

The positive interpellative possibilities of Paglia's work are brought into focus when compared with Canadian sexual assault law. Bill C-49, originally passed in 1992, seeks to clarify when consent has and has not been obtained so as to avoid instances of unjust sex and to help women gain convictions. It contains three major amendments: there is now a clearly defined legal definition of consent, the defence of "mistaken belief" has been narrowed, and there is statutory language around whether past sexual history is admissible.[26] Subsection 273.1(1) explains that "consent means ... the *voluntary* agreement of the complainant to engage in the sexual activity in question."[27] Subsection 273.1(2) defines contexts wherein no legal consent has been obtained. They include situations where consent is given by someone other than the complainant, where the complainant is unable to consent (for reasons of intoxication or otherwise), where the accused has obtained consent by abusing a position of trust or authority, where the complainant has expressed a lack of agreement (through words or otherwise), and where the complainant has expressed a desire to discontinue the activity in question.[28] These changes are particularly useful in criminalizing the procurement of nonvoluntary consent through a variety of means, including the common use of alcohol as a date rape drug.

Because law is constitutive of social relations, sociologist Kevin Bonnycastle argues, these seemingly benevolent reforms need to be examined more closely. He asks two important questions: "How is women's (and men's) subjectivity constituted in, and organized through, [the] (legal) rape text [and] how is this subjectivity channeled to other women and men?"[29] The prognosis for Bill C-49 is not good. In attempting to anticipate circumstances under which assault might occur, Bonnycastle explains that the reforms naturalize antiquated gender norms; they collude with gendered dualisms that write men as sexually aggressive and coercive and assaulted women as passive, powerless, and devoid of agency. In this way, he reasons, Bill C-49 assumes a certain sexual victimization of women and, in so doing, solidifies common sexual assault scripts. Here, "both 'the raped woman' and 'the rapist' always already exist within legal discourse" in limited and gendered ways.[30] Put another way, the bill interpellates gendered subjects into rather unfavourable gendered positions. When critical work does not first examine the categories and concepts used in its production, the power relations embedded within those categories and concepts tend to be reproduced.[31] In the case of Bill C-49, this lack of examination results in an inability to address the economic and political inequalities that create the social conditions that make women susceptible to sexual assault.[32] A similar criticism can be made of continuum theories of heterosexual violence more generally, no doubt.

But we are not only interpellated into gendered subject positions through social practice (sexual assault), law (sexual assault law), and theory (feminist theories of sexual assault); we are also interpellated into particular kinds of affective positions. This process can be explained through feminist literary scholar Sharon Marcus's argument that sexual assault is both scripted and scripting. The scripting is political when we think of the manner in which sexual assault writes on "men's and women's embodied selves and psyches the misogynist inequalities which enable rape to occur."[33] It is also affective in enacting "conventional, gendered structures of feelings and action."[34] Assault, Marcus explains, feminizes women as objects of male violence and *subjects of fear*. Sara Ahmed agrees that emotion secures and stabilizes social identities. "Emotions become attributes of collectives, which get constructed as 'being' through 'feeling.'"[35] Although Ahmed uses this idea to think about the formation of national/racialized identities, it can be used to theorize sexual assault as well. The etymological root of the terms "passion" and "passive," she explains, is the Latin word *passio*, used to denote suffering. "To be passive is to be enacted upon, as a negation that is already felt as suffering. The fear of passivity is tied to the fear of emotionality, in which weakness is defined in terms of a tendency to be shaped by others."[36]

In this way, it is not just that sexual assault feminizes through associations with passivity but also that it feminizes through fears associated with suffering assault – fears that are themselves sites of suffering. It is no wonder, then, why feminists reject conceptual practices that constitute women as subject to assault. This rejection works to remove emotional vulnerability from the passion/passivity/suffering triad and, in doing so, works against assault scripts. Put another way, to prevent being touched emotionally by avoiding theories and policies that render women subject to emotional injury is to prevent being touched physically in unfavourable ways.

Rejecting theories and policies that produce women as subject to assault, particularly those that rely upon and reinscribe unfavourable constructions of masculinity and femininity, is, as already alluded to, closely connected to rejecting the naming functions of assault more generally. For some, the coupling of assault with polarized gender positions through the language of dominance and submission might be the biggest risk associated with it. This argument is not to diminish the physical and psychological damage that assault can inflict but to argue that at least some of this injury arises on account of the social meanings attached to assault through its association with historical forms of political and economic disenfranchisement. Again, I am speaking of the interpellative functions of sexual assault, which call for a transformation not only of social practice but of theoretical practice as well.

Here, we can return to the difficulties of naming experience and refusals to label coercive sexual encounters as assault. Gavey provides the example of a man who does not listen to a woman's more subtle attempts to communicate a lack of interest in sex. She may become concerned that he will resort to using force and, as a result, acquiesce to coercive sex as a means of exercising a kind of constrained or strategic agency that saves her from having to conceive of the same experience as sexual assault.[37] In this case, she avoids the naming functions of assault, its gendering effects, and its attending stigmatization. Either-or conceptualizations of assault that are premised upon a constructed polarity between sex and violence, or erasures of date rape as seen in Paglia, facilitate this practice. Whereas continuum theories ensure that no instance of sexual violence goes unnoticed, either-or conceptualizations effect a kind of sanitation. But in removing ambiguity from the realm of sexual experience, either-or designations simultaneously limit the names we are able to adopt in the first place. Here, ambivalent encounters are pushed into one of two opposing camps, either normal sex or violent sexual assault, in a manner that does not always correlate with one's experience of the event in question. Just as discursive and experiential ambiguities create difficulties in naming experience, we find that our thinking/feeling interactions with sexual assault and textual representations of assault create difficulties in experiencing a name.

Affecting Sexual Politics
The tendency for feminists to use emotion in argumentation was particularly overt in 1960s consciousness-raising groups. Women gathered to share stories, feelings, and experiences, and through the process, they developed feminist politics – as captured in the now famous slogan "the personal is political." By making "connections between their experiences and feelings," Ahmed explains, women were empowered to "examine how such feelings were implicated in structural relations of power."[38] Here, positive feelings were equated with equitable, or at least politically neutral, experiences and social practices, whereas negative feelings were equated with experiences of sexism, practices of discrimination, or exclusionary and oppressive politics. Consciousness-raising groups have since fallen out of favour, but the explanatory power of personal experience – its narration and attending affective resonance – remains high. For many feminists, emotion continues to hold the status of truth.

Radical feminism has used negative affect to argue against the production and use of pornography. In *Only Words*, MacKinnon cites the negative emotional reactions women have to viewing, modelling, and acting in pornography to argue that it constitutes a real injury to women through the images and acts that it portrays. Contemporary radical feminist Robert Jensen agrees. The emotional harms that pornography inflicts, he contends, arise from the fact that pornography reduces women to humiliated objects for male pleasure. "It hurts to know that so much of the pornography that men are buying fuses sexual desire with cruelty"; "it hurts women, and men like it, and it hurts just to know that."[39] In the anthology *Not for Sale*, there is also a tendency to link pornography with emotional harm. Authors who identify as having worked as pornography models or as "prostitutes" cite histories of childhood sexual abuse, physical and/or sexual abuse by romantic partners, post-traumatic stress disorder from recent sexual assault(s), manipulation and coercion, abject poverty, or substance abuse as their primary impetus for entering sex work.[40] And finally, there is the well-known critique of pornography put forward in Bonnie Sherr Klein's 1981 film *Not a Love Story*. As articulated by Susanna Paasonen, "explanations ... voiced in the film ultimately connect to feelings of violation and hurt and produce a specific basis for knowledge over pornography."[41]

The tendency within anti-pornography feminism is to legitimize only those affective responses consistent with its own. Essentially, any response that is not clearly negative, Paasonen explains, implies "that the woman in question has no sense of her own worth or that she is otherwise misguided."[42] Anti-pornography feminism's association of pornography with "feelings of hurt, sadness, anger, frustration fear and nausea as well as the adjunct political arguments of exploitation, sexism, racism and misogyny as innate to pornography" has created a discursive/political climate wherein negative affect is the only "acceptable reaction to pornography."[43] The problem, here, is not the honesty with which the interviewed participants in *Not a Love Story*, *Not for Sale*, and *Only Words* express their feelings but the use of these expressed emotions as "evidence" without any further need for explanation.

But the use of affect in political argumentation is not unique to radical feminism; it can be found in sex-positive feminism as well. Here, the focus is on positive affect, which is politicized through ideas of empowerment, desire, and choice. This tendency is particularly evident in texts that "talk back" to radical and liberal feminist writings on pornography and sex work. Pornography writer Marcy Sheiner, for example, in discussing her early encounters with pornography, explains that what she expected to find degrading and repulsive she found exciting. Although she does note that pornography tends to script women as objects for male pleasure, she is defiantly unapologetic about its arousing power play wherein "people earn money by sexually entertaining those who can afford to pay for it."[44] Here, the disparity between featured entertainers and consumers – a disparity that radical feminism would identify as falling along gendered (and racialized or classed) lines – becomes secondary to pornography's exciting and arousing potential. Elizabeth Bernstein's more recent sociological study *Temporarily Yours* documents positive narratives sex workers tell of their profession. Whereas those coming from women working the streets are filled with violence perpetrated by "johns," "pimps," and the police, those told by women independently employed often use positive emotional descriptors to validate their choice of profession, including the development of self-esteem by learning to set personal boundaries, better self-care practices, and bodily acceptance.[45]

Here, we find similarities between anti-pornography and sex-positive feminism. Both of these feminisms use affect to establish the "truth" of pornography, and both discipline our affective response to cultural objects by dictating acceptable and unacceptable feelings. Affect is used in writings on pornography and sex work, as well as in narratives that workers tell of their profession, as a determinant of truth. It seems that sex-positive feminism, like radical feminism, makes use of antiquated standpoint epistemologies in its privileging of affect. But Paasonen identifies a tendency that is even more concerning. She argues that sex-positive feminism sometimes uses affect to silence political critiques that do not properly align with its project. Sexual pleasure, specifically female sexual pleasure, is often treated as a fetish object in sex-positive accounts of pornography and sex work that has a "magic power to disarm critique of representational conventions, structures of production and distribution."[46] Like the woman who betrays herself in popular pornographic representations of the "no" that eventually becomes a "yes," critiques of pornography and sex work become "useless, hypocritical, or even a form of intellectual dishonesty" in the face of sexual pleasure.[47] Interestingly, we find that affect is used to produce totalizing, one-dimensional argumentation not only in radical and sex-positive feminisms but also in patriarchal myths regarding female sexuality, as the previous example indicates.

The propensity for similar cultural objects to elicit radically different emotional responses deserves serious consideration. Although Eve Kosofsky Sedgwick would critique this position, one possible explanation lies in Ann Cvetkovich's view of affect as discursively constituted. For Cvetkovich, affect is not "a pre-discursive entity"; there is no essential "link between sensational events and bodily sensations" even though this situation is often obscured by the tendency to position affect as natural.[48] In this way, the same text can elicit contradictory emotional responses because we have access to bodily sensation and emotion only through discourse – discourse that, no doubt, shapes how we experience sensations and emotions. Furthermore, discourses concerning what positive and negative affect mean intersect with political and theoretical discourses used to understand whichever cultural product or practice is under evaluation. It is the naturalization of affect that enables these processes to go unnoticed and that allows affect to be used as an argumentative tool toward whatever political or theoretical ends the reader or writer desires. Rather than affect clarifying what constitutes "good" politics, one's conception of what constitutes good politics finds justification through affect while also being generative of affect. In other words, the politicization of affect always assumes that emotion is experienced prior to its being given a political value because the role that politics plays in the formation of affect is overlooked.[49] Here, the use of affect, emotion, or feeling as an argumentative tool is tautological in that it can only ever prove a conclusion that has already been derived; it proves to the reader or writer what one already knows. This becomes a political and theoretical disciplinary process when we are encouraged to feel particular emotions vis-à-vis particular objects and when the very possibilities of what is available to feel, including how emotions are delineated in relation to one another, are limited by the availability of current discourse.

Here, we might conclude that although affect's rhetorical effects are obvious enough, its legitimacy as a determinant of "correct" politics and theory is weak. We are unable to make sense of the world without affect in that it is a mediating factor in all interpretation, yet discursive understandings of affect empty it of stable meaning, making it ineffectual in telling us much of anything at all. But this reading of affect must be reconsidered in returning to questions of sexual assault. Legal scholar Peter M. Tiersma argues that with the exception of minors and perhaps persons with certain kinds of disabilities, consent is the distinguishing factor between sex and assault. Consent has displaced force and resistance as the distinguishing factor between sex and assault because relying on force risks vilifying rough consensual play, it does not adequately address circumstances where physical force is absent, and, most significantly, it places the onus on women to prove they properly resisted.[50] But because, according to Tiersma, consent puts the emphasis on one's state of mind, it is closely coupled with affect or feeling. One's state of mind is never simply a cognitive affair; it is shaped through the manner in which bodily sensation and emotion are interconstituted with thought. We might argue, then, that in sex there is a correlation between one's state of mind and the activity in question – perceived as a pleasure even when not physical – whereas in assault there is no such correlation but a disjuncture, which is sure to provoke an unenthusiastic emotional response even if the body has, what we might read as, a positive physiological response. Here, we return to the explanatory powers of emotion in that it would seem that sex, by definition, is linked with positive feelings, whereas assault is linked to those that are negative. We are forced to rethink either the status of affect, the status of consent, or both.

Sedgwick provides an alternative to Cvetkovich's reading of affect. She argues that within the current academic climate of anti-essentialist hegemony, affect tends to be characterized through digital models of on-off representation. It is either present or it is not, with little demarcation between differences in kind. Put another way, on-off frameworks overlook "qualitative differences among ... different affects" and thus risk turning "affects ... into Affect."[51] It is for this reason that Sedgwick borrows psychologist Silvan Tomkins' system of finitely many values – the strength of which involves the "ability to discuss *how things differentiate*."[52] Sedgwick writes, "It's like a scanner or copier that can reproduce any work of art in 256,000 shades of gray. However infinitesimally subtle its discrimination may be there are crucial knowledges it simply cannot transmit unless it is equipped to deal with the coarsely reductive possibility that red is different from yellow is different again from blue."[53] But this kind of qualitative distinction between different affects is not a simple reversion to essentialist thought. Sedgwick contends that affects may still have any object insofar as "affective amplification is indifferent to the means-end difference."[54] In other words, objects do not guarantee a particular affective response even if affects are qualitatively distinct. Ahmed echoes this position. The feelings we develop for, or in relation to, objects do not arise on account of the characteristics of objects themselves; "feelings instead take the 'shape' of the contact we have with objects."[55] Affects are produced and feelings are experienced on the basis of how we perceive the objects with which we come into contact. Here, we return to Ahmed's use of "impression" and its refusal to distinguish between bodily sensation, emotion, and thought. "Whether I perceive something as beneficial or harmful clearly depends upon how I am affected by something" – a perception that "involves thought and evaluation, at the same time that it is 'felt' by the body."[56] We can see, here, how Sedgwick's rereading of affects lends support to Tiersma's use of consent as the factor that distinguishes sex from assault. The self-referentiality of inherently differentiated affects, combined with their nonattachment to particular objects, enables us to validate women's subjective accounts of reality without reifying the meanings of sexual encounters. Affect, emotion, and bodily sensation remain significant in productions of social meaning. If this were not the case, desire, pleasure, and enthusiasm (as positive feelings) and fear, revulsion, and anger (as negative feelings) would cease to have a role in distinguishing between play and violence, between sex and sexual assault. But the clarification that differentiated affects provide does not solve the problems of experiential ambiguity or emotional ambivalence that can arise through the use of consent as a conceptual category.

Consensus and Its Affective Labours
As Gavey puts it, theorists across the feminist spectrum have critiqued consent as an "adequate standard for ethical sexual engagement."[57] According to MacKinnon consent reveals the normalization of unequal social expectations in heterosexuality. Because "sex is ordinarily accepted as something men do to women," consent is not a meaningful concept.[58] Coming from a poststructural perspective, Bonnycastle has his own concerns. Citing political theorist Wendy Brown's position that consent presupposes unequal relations and should thus be abandoned, he explains that "consent invokes an 'always already existing' power relationship wherein one person complies with, or permits, actions initiated by another."[59] This relationship, of course, is gendered since it is assumed that women surrender or submit to the desires of men, who, in turn, become fixed in the active position of forwarding proposals. Indeed, the concerns these writers voice find further justification in dictionary definitions of consent, which is often framed as

"voluntary agreement to or *acquiescence* in what *another proposes or desires; compliance,* concurrence, *permission.*"[60] Additional synonyms for "consent" include "understanding," "acquiescence," and "allowance."

The definitional shortcomings of consent are highlighted when compared with the term "consensus." Although both words come from the Latin *consentire*, their meanings have since diverged.[61] Consensus involves "agreement in feeling, sympathy; ... harmony, accord."[62] Its synonyms include "concurrence," "concord," "unison," and "unity."[63] Here, the embedded power differentials between actor and acted upon in consent are removed in that compliance, acquiescence, and permission simply do not meet the basic minimum requirements for consensus. Beyond full and equal agreement, beyond communication and negotiation, consensus requires co-authorship. In this way, women are clearly moved outside of limiting "yes"-"no" options and toward infinite, noncodified choice. In a parallel shift, the question of whether sex is wanted or unwanted turns to the multiple, intersecting questions of who, what, where, when, why, and perhaps most importantly, how. As a result, consensus seems to render impossible the inclusion of what Gavey describes as unjust sex within the category of "just" sex.

But consensus also gives an obvious nod to affects, emotions, and bodily sensations. As outlined in the *Canadian Oxford Dictionary*, *consentire* contains the root word *sentire*, which, like the French *sens*, means "to feel." Further, consensus was originally used to refer to "common feeling."[64] Returning to Ahmed, we are reminded that emotions and feelings are relational; they "involve (re)actions or relations of 'towardness' or 'awayness'" that reflect how we interpret the objects with which we come into contact.[65] In consensus, this relationally is compounded. We experience relations of towardness and awayness not only to sexual activities but also to our perception of our partner's relations of towardness or awayness to these same activities. In other words, because consensus emphasizes a concurrence in sentiment or a harmony in belief, a relation of towardness to sex is not enough. The other's relation of towardness or awayness to the object becomes its own object to which we relate. In consensus, as suggested, partners are united in *common feeling*. Here, we solve the problem raised by Tiersma concerning the ambiguity of consent in situations that do not involve explicit verbal communication. According to Ahmed, others can read our "affective stance" through the manner in which "emotions shape the very surfaces of our bodies."[66] Without diminishing the importance of clear communication, this is precisely consensus's project – to remain attentive to what is being said emotionally even in the absence of more overt cues. This is not to argue that it is somehow possible for partners to have the exact same reading of every sexual interaction. But although discrepancies of meaning are bound to occur, consensus reduces the probability that misreadings will result in the kinds of experiential/emotional ambiguities and ambivalences that raise the question of whether charges should be laid. The intersubjective, embodied, and affective reading practices that consensus strives for are never guaranteed in consent, and they are, of course, fully absent in assault. Here, we find that part of the problem with consent is that it tends toward "binary models of thinking that detach interpretation from sensation and the mental from the corporal."[67] It would not otherwise be possible to label sexual encounters that do not correlate with one's own or the other's state of mind as consensual. Consensus, conversely, performs an important affective/intellectual labour for sexual politics by promoting a thinking that remains inextricable from feeling.

Conclusion

Both either-or and continuum of violence frameworks have their shortcomings. Although locating assault along a continuum of heterosexual violence does not always allow for enough distinction between sex and assault – a distinction that is important if we are to respect heterosexual women's choices – it is able to account for experiential and discursive ambiguities within unequal social relations. Here, our impressions of sexual encounters are shaped not only by previous personal experience, collective histories, and cultural narratives but also by the manner in which certain objects of feeling stand in proximity to others. Within this schema, *naming experience* becomes difficult. Conversely, either-or theories of assault are unable to account for experiences that cannot be clearly placed within the category of assault but that ought not be considered just sex either. But because theories and policies focused on sexual assault are productive of gendered subjects, either-or frameworks have appeal despite their limited explanatory abilities. At least as articulated by Paglia, they secure a more optimistic view of female agency in conceptualizing female subjects as capable of self-defence without muddying "normal" heterosexual encounters in the waters between sex and assault. Here, we encounter the difficulties of *experiencing a name* – difficulties that can be alleviated through refusals to acknowledge susceptibilities to emotional and physical injuries that mobilize fear as a strategy for stabilizing the category of woman.

But whether we are discussing difficulties in naming experience or difficulties in experiencing a name, sexual assault remains an embodied practice; it is on the body that "cultural truths concerning men and women are written."[68] Beginning with embodiment, feminists are able to theorize the intricacies of how assault is experienced. Sexual assault constitutes an intimate attack on one's "embodied selfhood" and "subjective integrity"; it is an intersubjective practice premised upon a "denial of intersubjectivity."[69] That is because, at least temporarily, "intersubjectivity becomes a one-way street rather than the dynamic engagement that embodiment calls for."[70] Moving from an embodied intersubjective reading of assault to an embodied intersubjective reading of sex, we confirm the affirmative qualities of consensus as an alternative to consent. Consensus is intersubjective in its privileging of the other's relation of towardness to or awayness from the sexual encounter in question. It is embodied in emphasizing common feeling as the interconstitution of bodily sensation, emotion, and thought. Here, affect is neither fetishized as having a direct line to truth nor regarded as external to subjective interpretations of experience. The affective character of consensus means it effectively acknowledges that consent needs to be an integrated mind/body experience.[71] The benefits of Paglia's analysis pale in comparison. Returning to a discussion of heterosexual intercourse, we find that consensus allows for potential valuations of powerlessness and even humiliations of the self while rendering the discourse of intercourse-as-violation inert. The goal, of course, is not simply to diminish incidents of assault by substituting consensus for consent but also to eliminate sexual assault as an object of thought.

3

Heterosexist Pornographies and Sex Work
Transgression, Signification, and the Politics of Shame

When it comes to the politics of pornography and sex work, radical feminists are unequivocal abolitionists. That is because, as argued by Catharine MacKinnon, both practices are tied to the social, political, and economic domination of women by men. For starters, pornography and sex work are premised upon female poverty; "women need to be kept poor so that they will be compelled to be available for money to any man who wants to buy them for sex."[1] Pornography and sex work further normalize the view of women as "sexual things" to be used for male enjoyment, according to MacKinnon. This kind of thingification is synonymous with femininity; to be properly feminized *is* to be properly objectified. There is no distinction to be made between alienation and objectification under patriarchal social conditions because – unlike men, who do not experience exploitation until their labour, objectified in products, is alienated from them – "women have not authored objectifications, we have been them."[2] She *is* the commodity, whether it is her body or image that is being sold.

Sex-positive feminists take a different tack. They reject singular readings that equate pornography with patriarchy and sex work with victimhood. Instead, they enact what could be called a discursive reversal; what was bad for the radical feminist becomes good for the sex-positive feminist. The Feminist Porn Awards, for example, do so by focusing on diverse sexualities and sexual representations. Here, criticisms of pornography as heteronormative and sexist are rendered inert, as only works that trouble hegemonic tropes and stereotypes are given airplay. Or, as they quote feminist porn star Annie Sprinkle, "the answer to bad porn isn't no porn ... it's to try and make better porn!"[3] Maggie's: The Toronto Sex Workers Action Project also provides a discursive reversal; it rewrites sex work as "socially legitimate, important and valuable."[4] The problem with sex work, for Maggie's, is not that it is inherently oppressive and damaging for practitioners and society; the problem is discrimination, stigmatization, and criminalization.[5] Under the recent Conservative government, Maggie's turned its efforts toward fighting against Bill C-36, which criminalizes the purchase of sexual services, because it contends that the bill fails to adequately address the safety needs of sex workers.[6]

Here, I explore some of the limitations of sex-positive feminists' argumentation concerning pornography and sex work. But instead of focusing on where their analyses go wrong (which would be out of line with the aim of the book), I investigate how sex-positive argumentation operates for readers. The political implications of theorizing pornography and sex work as repressed and in need of liberation can be read through Michel Foucault's critique of the repressive hypothesis. In doing so, we find that the sex-positive feminist fight against repression works to position sex-positive thinkers as transgressive while overlooking the actual content of what is "liberated." The content in which I am primarily interested includes pornographic practices of representation as well as sex work as a representational practice, both of which I theorize through psychoanalytic theories of desire. Desire occurs through processes of fantasy and signification only loosely tied to the objects toward which it is directed. At the same time, desire necessitates that identification with the image or practice has already taken place. Identification shapes the relationships we form to feminist arguments and frameworks used to analyze pornography and sex work. When pornography and sex work are theorized through the affect of shame, we find that shame informs our attachments and detachments not only to images and practices but also to the arguments and frameworks that we use to understand them.

Producing Transgressive Subjects

Sex-positive feminism's interest in renaming pornography and sex work practices is closely tied to projects of resisting repression. The Feminist Porn Awards, for example, rescript explicit sexual representation by giving voice to genders and sexualities that have been marginalized by traditional heteronormative pornographies. Maggie's, similarly, rewrites sex work by fighting against laws and social practices that attempt to restrict or control the free selling and purchasing of sexual services. The emphasis on resisting repression is particularly evident in sex-positive writings that emerged out of the feminist sex wars. This work typically positions itself against radical feminism's perceived alignment with the Christian right and conservative morality.[7] As the argument against repression goes, since sex is pleasurable and female sexuality has been disproportionately repressed, female sexual empowerment requires liberation from repression, whether it is straight, queer, monogamous, polyamorous, vanilla, kinky, or explicitly commodified. Sex radical Gayle Rubin, for example, argues that sexual repression has created an erotic pyramid, with married, heterosexual, monogamous, reproductive couples at the top and polyamorous queers, transsexuals, "transvestites," fetishists, BDSM practitioners, and sex workers at the bottom.[8] For sex-worker rights activist Priscilla Alexander, stigma and repression have been present in almost every century on almost every continent, which potentially explains why sex work continues to be prohibited despite copious documentation detailing how this negatively affects women.[9] According to famous pornography producer and director Candida Royalle, repression stems from male fear of female sexual power and is used as a means of controlling women.[10] Former sex worker and relationship coach Veronica Monet proposes sedition as an antidote to repression and social prohibition in order to help "incite others to rebel against ... the standards ... used to control women's sexual behavior."[11] And self-defined "sexpert" Susie Bright argues that "sexual speech ... is the most repressed and disdained kind of expression in our world."[12]

What we see is that sex-positive feminism has a long history of positioning sex and sexuality as subject to repression.[13] But in resisting repression, sex-positive feminism buys into the repressive hypothesis.

As explained by Foucault, the dominant, albeit incorrect, view of the relation between sexuality and society from the seventeenth century onward has been that of repression.[14] "According to the repressive hypothesis ... the history of sexuality could only be that of the 'negative relation' between power and sex, of 'the insistence of the rule,' of 'the cycle of prohibition,' of 'the logic of censorship,' and of 'the uniformity of the apparatus' of scarcity."[15] Here, sexualities and sexual practices outside bourgeois, conservative law supposedly fell into obscurity, Foucault explains; there was simply nothing to say, see, or know. Liberating sexuality, then, would necessitate radical social transformation. "Nothing less than a transgression of laws, a lifting of prohibitions, an irruption of speech, a reinstating of pleasure within reality, and a whole new economy in the mechanisms of power [would] be required."[16]

But, of course, Foucault tells us that the repressive hypothesis is a misrepresentation of the relationship between sexuality and power. It is not that we have always been free from prohibitions on sex; it is that prohibition cannot be understood as *the* defining feature of sex these past few hundred years.[17] Instead, he argues, we have seen a proliferation of sexual discourse; the past three centuries have witnessed a rise in the variety and dispersion of devices "for speaking about [sex], for having it be spoken about, for inducing it to speak of itself."[18] Emerging from institutional apparatuses, these (often radically varied) discourses emerged concurrently, all striving to reveal, and often claiming to have, the truth about sex.[19] They "did not multiply apart from or against power, but in the very space and as the means of its exercise."[20] In other words, sex has been administered though regulatory discourse, not taboo.

If it is the case that we have witnessed a proliferation of discourse, not totalizing repression, we must ask why so many of us continue to be invested in the repressive hypothesis. As Foucault puts it, "the question ... is not, Why are we repressed? but rather, Why do we say, with so much passion and so much resentment against our more recent past, against our present, and against ourselves, that we are repressed?"[21] There might be two reasons. The first, suggested by Foucault, is that an investment in the repressive hypothesis is for the benefit of the speaker. If sex is repressed, he explains, then speaking about it becomes a pleasurable form of transgression – an anticipation of a coming freedom or a speaking-out against the powers that be. Here, sex-positive feminism can position itself as a daring harbinger of liberation. We need only look at the titles of a few sex-positive texts focused on pornography or sex work to see this dynamic at play: Pamela Church Gibson and Roma Gibson's *Dirty Looks,* Jill Nagle's *Whores and Other Feminists,* Shannon Bell's *Whore Carnival,* and more recently, Katrien Jacobs, Marije Janssen, and Matteo Pasquinelli's *C'Lick Me*.[22] As readers, we are positioned similarly. When we sit in the library or on the bus with one of these titles, we enact pleasurable transgressions of our own. We become the harbinger of liberation, resisting a culture that would stigmatize or repress diverse female sexual expressions. This playful transgression comes further into focus when contrasted with radical feminist titling practices. Andrea Dworkin's work provides quintessential examples: *Women Hating, Our Blood, Letters from a War Zone,* and *Heartbreak,* the last published a few years before her death.[23] Here, instead of sexualizing the reader in opposition to patriarchal practices of repression, these titles, from a sex-positive feminist perspective at least, inadvertently intensify repressive social norms. Rather than positioning the reader as resisting repression, they position her as a militant ideologue.

The second reason sex-positive feminism might be invested in discourses of repression is that they facilitate the creation of divisions between feminisms that are supposedly forward-thinking in their celebration of diverse sexual expressions and those that remain stuck within a critique of sexual representations and practices. A dualism is created that places liberatory feminism on one side and backward ideologies and feminisms that continue to enact the logic of repression, particularly with regard to pornography and sex work, on the other. Here, we are reminded of sex-positive feminism's concern with radical feminism's circumstantial alignment with conservative Christianity. Numerous differences between the Christian right and radical feminism are eclipsed as they come to occupy the same discursive space. In this way, sex-positive feminism is able to label radical feminism anti-sex – a euphemism for bad feminisms that inadvertently enact punishments on women merely trying to exercise their sexual agency and shed the repressive chains of a patriarchal culture. In fact, it is by labelling some feminisms anti-sex that sex-positive feminism is able to take on the sex-positive designation in the first place.[24] Interestingly, sex-positive feminism's characterization of radical feminism as moralistic does not consider its own moral imperative, namely to throw off the yoke of repressive social norms.

These two motivations for resisting repression – as a form of transgression and as a means of creating feminist divisions – are indeed connected. Transgression is defined as an "infringement or violation of a law, command, or duty"; to transgress is to offend by going against an established code of conduct.[25] Put another way, it is to fall out of line with the dominant social order. But, of course, when the dominant social order is seen as unnecessarily restrictive or unjust, transgression becomes liberatory. And because sex-positive feminism practises transgression by resisting repression, identifying with sex-positive feminism can solidify a reader's feminist credentials. This dynamic is compounded through sex-positive vilifications of radical feminism. Worse than being rejected by the academy, radical feminists have been stereotyped as irrational and man-hating by gender conservatives. In contrast, sex-positive feminists are interpellated as rational and fun – as the good feminists who will stand up for sexual pleasure against both conservatives and feminist killjoys, especially if it means engaging in and celebrating transgressive sexualities and sexual practices.

The Limits of Resisting Repression

Perhaps counterintuitively, radical feminism also positions itself as resisting repression. This time, however, the oppressive force is patriarchal social relations, not a sex-negative society that stigmatizes all expressions of female sexual pleasure. For radical feminists, it is not that women have not had enough access to sex but that they have had too much – too much sex on male terms by way of sexual objectification, sexual harassment, and sexual assault. Here, the focus is on the *quality*, not the *quantity*, of sex and sexuality. In other words, as the argument goes, any attempt to liberate heterosexual female sexuality needs to focus on the discursive terms on which it is understood rather than on the quantity of its expressions. It is patriarchy that has negatively affected the quality of heterosexual sex for women and stigmatized queer sexual expressions.[26] In this way, radical feminism places sex on the agenda for the future – a postpatriarchy future where sex will finally be enjoyable for women (and men) once women are able to articulate sex on their *own* terms. For radical feminists, because pornography and sex work are intimately tied to patriarchal social relations, these practices also need to be abolished in order for sex to be good. Here, the repressive hypothesis serves radical feminism's political program. Readers are positioned as "being in the know," as not having been fooled by patriarchy's attempts to disguise inequality as simply sex. Heterosexual subjects are then empowered to avoid or to be very cautious of heterosexual encounters until the work of overthrowing patriarchy has been completed. In this way, radical feminism could be said to encourage transgressions of its own insofar as heterosexuality is encouraged, if not compulsory, under male supremacy.[27]

Although there are reasons to be cautious of radical feminism's project, the reasons for paying heed to the quality of liberated discourses and practices find elucidation when we look at the *kinds* of narratives that have proliferated on sex and sexuality these past fifty years. Two of the most vital centres for the production of discourse concerning specifically female sexuality during this time have been feminism and pornography. Feminism, as we know, has produced a large body of varied and contradictory knowledges. But although feminist knowledges might not always agree, they work to similar ends: substantive female sexual equality and meaningful sexual choice.[28] Pornographic discourse has been less diverse. There has been a recent increase in the quantity and visibility of queer and feminist productions, as seen in the example of the Feminist Porn Awards, but mainstream commercial pornography continues to reproduce a limited and limiting display of scripted genders and sexualities. These pornographic knowledges tend to be, in the words of sociologist Simon Hardy, "predicated on the symbolic power of men over women."[29] Put another way, they are aligned with heterosexist discourse; mainstream pornography normalizes male dominance/activity/subjecthood and female submission/passivity/objecthood through representations and discourses that stabilize gendered and sexual binaries while marginalizing diversity.[30] This tendency in mainstream pornography, not surprisingly, precludes easy partnership with feminism.

The limited liberatory potential of pornographic discourse can be seen in the recent rise of user-generated pornography sites such as Xtube, PornoTube, RedTube, YouPorn, XHamster, Xvideos, and PornHub.[31] Whereas for years feminist discussions of pornography took the form of heated debate, an emerging body of literature, indebted to sex-positivism, focuses on pornography practices in relation to changing media trends.[32] Media theorist Sharif Mowlabocus, for instance, cautiously suggests that user-generated sites might contribute to a democratization of sexual representation. In blurring the lines between producer, performer, distributor, and consumer, they allow for more user participation and content control.[33] Actors are able to interact with fans, fans are able to interact with other users, and there is a more direct line of payment between those making work and those consuming it. In addition, by providing a platform for amateurs to showcase their talent, the sites enable more gender and sexual diversity.[34] In other words, these pornographies offer the potential to resist heterosexist representation without falling into censorship or the supposed politics of repression.

But as much as these sites might offer a potential democratization of pornography, they also provide a continuation of heterosexist discourse. Video clips that involve male dominance and female submission are still prevalent on user-generated sites. And like pornographies featured in more traditional media, they seldom employ the kinds of signifiers or dialogue that might communicate to the viewer that the scene in play is a negotiated fantasy.[35] The pre-scripted theatrical roles are neither interchangeable on the basis of gender nor transparently positioned as fantasy. When pornographic content is framed as devoid of egalitarianism but not also framed as theatre, the distinction between camp and mimetic representation breaks down. And, when this occurs, performances of dominance and submission can become naturalized as synonymous with heterosexual sex itself. In other words, the dominance and submission are easily read through heterosexual discourse as opposed to BDSM discourse, which would render it democratic.

The other way these sites reproduce heterosexist discourse is through the structuring of the user interface that allows viewers to search for videos, comment on or rate videos, as well as categorize, title, and tag posts.

Whereas Mowlabocus applauds the manner in which video tagging by users can mean that searches yield a variety of body types and levels of professionalization, I am more skeptical. With the exception of penis size and racial identification, one can rarely specify male physical attributes in straight search engines. Instead, videos are organized according to female physical attributes such as body type, breast size, hair colour, race, pubic hair maintenance, age, sexual experience, and so on. Even if viewers do tag videos in ways that are not heterosexist, the structuring of the sites curtails our access to this potential subversion. In this way, user-generated pornography sites, like most heteronormative pornography, continue to assume, interpellate, and privilege a male heterosexual viewer. It seems, then, as with the related so-called revolution in Internet content more generally, that user agency is limited.[36] When proponents of these new technologies do not maintain a cautious optimism, they may inadvertently allow for the reproduction of the very discourses they are trying to fight against.

The problem of reproducing heterosexism under the guise of resisting repression is even more evident in writer and self-described "professional sexual deviant" Eva Pendleton's piece "Love for Sale," written at the end of the feminist sex wars.[37] She argues that the category of the good wife rests on "the spectre of unchastity" and is constructed in opposition to the "whore."[38] In this way, the stigmatization of sex workers indirectly reinforces "white [middle-class] procreative heterosexuality."[39] When sex work is no longer stigmatized, we find that it constitutes a queer practice that troubles heterosexuality, according to Pendleton. This effect is evident when looking at lesbian-identified sex workers who provide services to male clients; for Pendleton, they demonstrate the extent to which *all* sex work is a performance of heterosexuality. Put another way, "sex work is drag" – a "mimetic performance of highly charged ... gender codes" often involving female "sexual availability and feminine receptivity."[40] Sex work further provides an "indictment of gender roles by demanding payment for playing them."[41] Pendleton concludes that sex work is, then, generally advantageous for women, whether they are working in the industry or not, because it queers heteronormativity, destabilizes heterosexuality, provides a basis for revaluations of gender, proliferates sexual "deviances," and refuses the norms that govern "proper" female sexual conduct.[42]

But, as we saw with pornography, Pendleton's analysis of sex work may allow for a continuity of the very discourses she seeks to disrupt. According to legal scholar Jane Scoular, sex work is best "viewed with ambivalence"; "it is an activity which challenges the boundaries of heterosexist, married monogamy but may also be an activity which reinforces the dominant norms of heterosexuality and femininity."[43] To my mind, Scoular's point finds support through the work of lawyer and feminist author Thomas Macaulay Millar in two ways. First, Millar argues that our culture is one where sex is "a thing" that women have and men try to get. When sex is conceived of as a commodity that can be "given, bought, sold, or stolen," it is not uncommon for women to do what they can to increase the value of this commodity on the market.[44] This undertaking might be seen among sex workers who position themselves as servicing only executives but also, as Millar argues, in the seemingly disparate celibacy movement.[45] By refusing to have premarital sex, heterosexual girls and women work to trade their "commodity" for "the best possible gain" – in this case, marriage.[46] Insofar as sex work also ascribes to discourses that position sex as a commodity, it fails to destabilize normative white, middle-class female heterosexualities and, in fact, might even reproduce them. The second way that sex work reproduces heteronormativity is by inadvertently repositioning women as disproportionately subject to sexual assault. For Millar, when sexual encounters are framed as being analogous to property transactions, things quickly become unethical.[47] Property transactions are not always uniformly advantageous because they depend on bargaining power, which varies on the basis of one's social position, Millar explains. More importantly, property transactions do not require enthusiastic consent; "a deal is a deal, however reluctantly, grudgingly, or desperately one side accepts it."[48] This is to say that consensus is not the basic minimum requirement for a deal to be considered legitimate, raising the spectre of discursive ambiguities and experiential ambivalences in sex (or assault). The argument, here, is not to conflate voluntary with forced labour, as radical feminism has done, but to think critically about the manner in which discourses that position female sexuality as an object of exchange might lend support to discourses that constitute women as subject to assault. Simply put, if something can be sold, it can also be stolen.[49]

Both these arguments force us to reconsider Pendleton's argument that sex work troubles heteronormative femininity. Although she is right to argue that femininity in sex work is performed, we are reminded of Judith Butler's contention that performances work only to the extent that they produce "naturalized effects" and "compel belief."[50] This outcome is necessary in order that the performance might be socially intelligible as a kind of sexualized femininity. Put another way, performances of femininity function in sex work only to the extent that they are *not* explicitly read as performance.[51] Although Pendleton does acknowledge that "the concept of sex as a commodity sold by women and consumed by men is something that bears further feminist analysis," we might also point out the obvious fact that being paid to play sexualized gender roles is itself a gendered role.[52] Insofar as it is a continuity of how cisgendered women have been traditionally understood, we can conclude that sex work does not queer heterosexuality but has been integral to it.

Essentially, feminist arguments that link resisting repression to liberation divert attention away from the *content* of what is being liberated; when overcoming repression becomes a central feminist goal, examining the social meanings, historical investments, and political implications of what is emancipated can become secondary. In this way, sex-positive feminism runs the risk of presenting a continuity of previously established discourses or even condoning heteronormativity when honouring representations or social practices simply because they exceed the bounds of repressive social norms or provide an alternative to secrecy and moral condemnation.[53] Without wanting to undermine sex-positive feminism's important contributions, particularly with regard to the destigmatization of sex workers and the celebration of diverse pornographies, it is important to acknowledge that representations of female sexuality and sexual practices performed by women are not *necessarily* positive or immune to social critique. Their production through and of discourse must remain a central focus so as not to acquiesce to the very problems feminists seek to address.

In fact, it may even be that feminist arguments that position themselves against sexual repression are tied to the proliferation of conservative discourse. Resisting repression is often positioned as a transgressive act. But as feminist legal scholar Alex Dymock contends, transgression can create only short-lived experiences of freedom; what it actually does is resist social transformation.[54] That is because, as I interpret things, discourses that address repression allow institutionally located sexual discourses to proliferate in the shadows. Pornography, for example, continues to be constructed as somewhat illicit despite its widespread accessibility and the normalization of its use. Pornographers and users invest in this construction so as to produce its production and consumption as a kind of low-risk transgression. But insofar as the sexualities and sexual practices in mainstream pornography exist according to narrow discursive terms, this transgression, like all transgressions, easily operates as an indirect reverence for the law.[55] In the case of sex work, sex-positive feminism's irregular positioning of sex workers as an erotic group or as outlaws does not contribute to a proliferation of sexual deviance, as Pendleton suggests, but might actually limit resignification by reaffirming the kind of normative heterosexuality that sex work supposedly rebels against.[56] Here, buying into the repressive hypothesis becomes a means through which interpretive fields are "stratified by specific modes of recontextualization," to use the language of communications and performance studies professor Nina Philadelphoff-Puren.[57] The repressive hypothesis obscures the manner in which hegemonic understandings of sexuality and gendered difference continue to have an unfair advantage in shaping how the inherently "multi-vocal and polyvalent" text is received. As a result, it can inadvertently recreate the narrowly defined discursive terms that produce the felt need to fight against repression in the first place.[58]

Desire, Fantasy, and Signification

Although it is easy to critique sex-positive feminism for overlooking the content of what is liberated when overthrowing repressive sexual norms, it is also the case that the social meaning of any particular content cannot be guaranteed. This is particularly the case when it comes to the politics of desire. The tendency, however, has been to read desire in a one-to-one relation in both pornography and sex work. Put more clearly, the tendency has been to assume that pornography and sex work excite on the basis of exactly what is seen or experienced as if the image or act in question could have only one meaning. In opposition to these readings, psychoanalytic film critic Elizabeth Cowie explains that the "object does not cause the desire."[59] Desire exists, rather, in relation to systems of signification both in terms of how objects of desire are signified socially and in terms of how that social signification is of psychic significance to the subject. To simply assume, instead, that arousal is produced on account of a literal reading of the narratives displayed or enacted "effaces the complex system of signification involved and the complex fantasy implied."[60] "What arouses is already a highly coded entity," and sexual arousal is principally "a psychical relation."[61] Simply put, desire is first co-opted to fantasy, not the object, so any arousal experienced occurs on account of the fantasy scenario presented, Cowie explains.

It is further the case that fantasy, like the Freudian dream, is subject to condensations, reversals, and displacements; fantasy is bound up with internal conflicts and knotted into emotional investments. In this way, as argued by psychoanalytic literary critic Jacqueline Rose, it is not just that sexuality is located in the "subjectivity of the viewer" rather than in the content of what the subject views but also that the "relationship between viewer and scene is always one of fracture, partial identification, pleasure and distrust."[62] For Cowie, this situation suggests that the objects found in the fantasy scenario may stand in precisely for what they are not or as "substitutes in the process of defense."[63] An example can be seen in socialist feminist Lynne Segal's reading of popular pornographic tropes. It is easy to interpret images of "the ubiquitously sexually desiring, visibly sexually satisfied female ... the huge, hard, magical male member – always erect, forever unflagging ... [and] two or more men engaged in joint sex with one woman" as premised upon a desire to group assault a sexually objectified and accessible woman through the phallus as weapon.[64] Segal, instead, reads these tropes as a means through which the fictitiousness of such discourses are (thinly) veiled; "do we not see only too clearly here fear of female rejection, terror of phallic failure, and homosexual feeling disguised as heterosexual performance?"[65] Cowie provides her own example, this time examining the complicated ways that viewers might identify with the scene portrayed:

> The figures in the scene stand for positions of desire: to love or be loved from this place, to pleasure or be pleasured from this position ... Hence a man may identify with the woman's pose of self-display [her genitals exposed for the camera] insofar as it signifies the wish to be found lovable in one's sex, an identification with a passive wish, rather than an identification with the woman and her body as female.[66]

Again, the heterosexed male viewer is not aroused on account of the sexually available woman, as radical feminism would argue, but as "an identification with the exhibitionism of the scene."[67] Here, Cowie contends, the woman's body comes to act as the sign of his desire to be desired.

But how can we apply Cowie's and Segal's analyses concerning the uncertainty of the pornographic object of desire to sex work? It is rather easy to interpret desire as operating in sex work toward a reification of biological difference. The gender of service providers is not interchangeable for clients unless, of course, they already have flexible object choice. For heterosexual male clients looking to pay for sex (heteroflexible, bi, or trans lovers aside), a *necessary* condition of the job for a service provider is that she be a cisgendered female. Here, gendered/sexed identity is non-negotiable in a way that is not true for most other kinds of labour. We could note exceptions – surrogate mothering, wet nursing, sperm and egg donation – except that sex work is tied to gendered biology on the basis of sexual desire. In this way, sex work constitutes a unique labour practice that is not only mediated by biological difference and desire but also seems to be productive of biological difference through desire.

If investigations of fantasy in pornography (as a representational practice) demonstrate the nonlinearity of desire, the same argument must be made of sex work (as a practice subject to representation). Just as the viewer's relationship to the image can never be definitely determined, so too is that true of the client's relationship to the sexual fantasy presented by, or co-created with, the sex worker. What arouses is the psychic significance the fantasy scenario holds for the client. This is to say that even if desire appears to operate in sex work toward reifications of biological difference, that is not necessarily what is happening for the client on a conscious or, more significantly, unconscious level.[68] And this is a good thing considering that arguments that read desire as reifying biology in sex work would have negative consequences for all sexual desire. Desire exists in connection to sexed difference as mediated by gendered discourse whether that difference is marked similarly or dissimilarly from our own.[69] If we were to reject desire on the basis of its relationship to biology and gendered discourse in sex work, we would need to reject all sexual desire flat out.

But with both pornography and sex work, there is still reason for caution. The fantasy scenario does not provide an endless array of options; it constitutes a "textually orchestrated ... limited set of oppositions, which the spectator must enter, and hence psychically be able to enter, or else the scenario will 'fail' for him" or her.[70] In this way, even though the relation between desire and signification can never be known in advance, certain scenarios might still be more readily available to some subjects than others.[71] Radical feminism can read the relation between pornography, sex work, and fantasy in an overdetermined manner. Kate Millett, for example, argues that patriarchal social relations are what enable women to identify as sex workers or to enter the fantasy scenario as sellers of sexual services. Subjection to physical, emotional, and sexual abuse prepares her for a life of prostitution, in which her sexual being is not constructed for her own pleasure.[72] But arguments that draw causal lines between the social construction of subjects and the fantasy scenario effectively eliminate the element of choice. Choice is critically important in shaping our subjective impression of an experience; it is what distinguishes a job from abduction, sex from assault, motherhood from childbearing as depicted in Margaret Atwood's novel *The Handmaid's Tale*.[73] As a result, it is important to balance the specificity of how the subject has been socially constituted with individual agency. Because ideology still has a bearing on identity formation and because desire never escapes the purview of the unconscious, we return to the idea that choices are unevenly desired on the basis of their accessibility to different subjects. Internalized social scripts shape our understandings of self and, in turn, the choices we make.[74] When we fetishize choice, we erase the relationship between interiority and the social through which subjectivity is formed.[75]

Shame and Theories of Pornography and Sex Work

Here, I want to think about three things: how affect and processes of identification shape the relationships that readers form to pornography and sex-work practices; the fantasies that feminists can hold regarding the consumption of pornography and sex work by others; as well as how the relationships that feminist thinkers form to theories used to analyze pornography and sex work are mediated by the politics of shame. The social constitution of the subject is not the only thing lubricating one's relationship to the fantasy scenario. Affect plays a significant role as well. That is because, as Susanna Paasonen explains, affect is always present in processes of interpretation: "Working with affect means acknowledging moments of being impressed or overwhelmed by images [or practices], their power to resist attempts at readerly … mastery, the ways in which images [and practices] move and resonate with the bodies of those facing them, as well as how these movements figure in the interpretations and theorizations made."[76] Insofar as our interpretative relations are always mediated by affect, Paasonen continues, texts are both affecting and effecting. This is particularly the case with pornography and sex work. Pornography is designed to transmit "sensations and affective intensities"; it is designed to move consumers in "highly bodily ways."[77] Like melodrama, comedy, and horror films, it seeks to evoke emotional responses in its viewers that are similar to those depicted in the text.[78] Likewise, sex work is a social practice organized around affect. Akin to psychotherapy, spiritual leadership, politics, nursing, early childhood education, or flight attending, the job demands affective mastery. If the service providers do not effectively nurture appropriate affective states in the clients, they have failed at their job, and it is unlikely the clients will seek out their services again.

The affective relationships we develop to images and practices are also shaped by processes of identification. As articulated by art historian

Amelia Jones, "we attach to or repel ourselves from images (and bodies in general) through complex and shifting circuits of identification and disidentification."[79] This circumstance is, of course, aligned with what we have been discussing all along, namely that our intellectual relationships to the world are always interested – an interest that stems as much from how we see ourselves reflected or not reflected in the world as it does from our political commitments. Put another way, we develop likes and dislikes with regard to the world and its objects on the basis of how we imagine or fantasize our own relationship to them.[80] Cultural critic Laura Kipnis's analysis of the pornographic magazine *Hustler* provides an example. She contends that feminist rejections of hardcore pornography have as much, or more, to do with its working-class aesthetic as they do with misogyny.[81] Put another way, feminists reject *Hustler* on the basis of how they imagine themselves in relation to the text they are evaluating. Here, readers disidentify with the magazine's working-class connotations to position themselves as educated and as having the social capital to immunize themselves against its seductiveness. Liking the magazine, in this scenario, might conflict with their sense of self.

The affective relationships we have to texts, as mediated by processes of identification, further provide clues to why the terrain is so fraught for feminist thinkers. Yes, consumers of pornography and sex work develop fantasized relationships to the objects of their consumption, but so too do feminists. More convoluted are the fantasized relationships that feminists develop to the relationships consumers form to pornography and sex work. Just as the viewer's or client's relations to images and practices are shaped by desire as complicated by processes of signification, so too is that no doubt true of the feminist reader's understanding of how others consume them. Here, we find that the relationships feminist readers form to pornography and sex work are often shaped by how much credit they lend the consumer.[82] Sex-positive feminists are likely to imagine consumers as having a decent level of visual, cultural, and political literacy and as occupying a variety of gendered social positions. This is to say that if a pornographic scene involves an unnegotiated power play or tired gender roles, the sex-positive reader is more inclined to assume that viewers have the competence to read the image as a representation of fantasy. The same goes for sex work where the sex-positive feminist is prone to read the consumers as cognizant of the fact that they are buying a sexual service from workers whose own sexual preferences may not be aligned with the services offered. Radical feminists, conversely, tend to imagine consumers of pornography and sex work in a more limited way. Here, the fantasy is that the consumer is almost always a cisgendered male who lacks the literacy to read complicated images or practices as anything other than a reflection of his preconceived gender biases and inegalitarian views of sexuality. Given the constructed opposition between rational thought and emotion, it may also be that radical feminists hold these practices in suspicion because they assume consumers will be so easily duped by them.

It is not just that affect and identification shape interpretive practices and that feminists fantasize the consumption of pornography and sex work in particular ways; it is also that shame complicates the relationships that feminists form to theories used to analyze these two practices. My contention is that we form relationships to feminist arguments and frameworks used to analyze the politics of pornography and sex work as a means of negotiating shame. Queer cultural theorist Sally Munt borrows Charles Darwin's description of shame as involving "a strong desire for concealment" from the gaze of others.[83] For Darwin, the attentions we receive can incite shame as we evaluate how others evaluate us. We are particularly weary of the evaluative gaze levelled at our personal appearance and moral conduct, Munt continues. It is not surprising, then, that pornography and sex work are often tied to shame insofar as they are both areas where appearance and moral conduct are judged. One way evaluations of personal appearance are experienced is on the basis of embodied difference. The body can been seen only within its specificity, but we are brought into existence according to discursive terms that were never of our own choosing. If we identify with the gendered presentation of the body displayed or employed in the pornographic or sex-work scene, shame might arise from feelings of misrecognition or, alternatively, as a desire to conceal that which cannot be concealed. Even though it might not be one's own embodiment or personal appearance that is being evaluated, a reader's identification with the gendered presentation of a practitioner might evoke feelings of shame. Evaluations of morality also evoke shame through processes of identification. Radical feminists, for example, project shame outward onto the male dominance that has forced women, either overtly or through economic constraint, into said practices. It is essential that blame be transferred to patriarchy as well as to male producers, managers, and consumers in order to ensure the sexualized female subject is not read as morally culpable. Here, processes of disidentification are at play.[84] The same is true of sex-positive feminists who attempt to distance themselves from the shaming strategies of radical feminism by turning what was a site of moral condemnation into one of pride. People tend to experience shame whenever something that they are interested in is criticized, geographer and feminist theorist Elspeth Probyn explains; shame is a response to thwarted interest.[85] This situation could explain the intense response some sex-positive feminists have to anti-pornography and anti-sex-work feminism; not only are they shamed for their "inadequate" moral stance, but their interest has also been interrupted and laid bare.

But shame is not only tied to appearance and morality, Munt explains; it is also "organized around issues of attachment and detachment."[86] That is because, as I contend, shame is a faith-based affect. For Sigmund Freud, beliefs are established through libidinal cathexis.[87] To cathect with a person, object, or idea is to develop an attachment, and attachment is always intimately connected with identification. We cathect to objects that either reflect characteristics of the self or reflect characteristics that are missing in the self. Experiences of shame, in this way, indicate that cathexis/attachment and, therefore, identification have already taken place. There needs to be an identification with the desirable or undesirable in order for the stigmatization of falling short of the ideal to have an emotional impact on us – in order that we might recognize the properties of the undesirable as associated with the self. Here, we find that theorists develop attachments to arguments and frameworks used to theorize pornography and sex work on the basis of beliefs they may not consciously control. In this light, some thinkers might be attracted to the epistemic certainty of radical feminism because it responds to an affective need for truth that the theorist has come to believe is necessary to feminism. Sex-positive feminists, when influenced by poststructural thinking, are more likely to argue that the meaning of any speech cannot be overdetermined.[88] Here, the appeal might be a lack of epistemic certainty or an internalized belief that the theorist cannot know the truth of any image or practice definitively. Both certainty and equivocal meaning can be a means of negotiating shame. Attaching oneself to theories that purport to know the patriarchal truth of pornography and sex work avoid shame by positioning the theorist as superior and omnipotent. Adhering to equivocal meaning avoids shame by evading the exposure of one's political position in order to eliminate the possibility that one's position might be proved wrong.

Conclusion

In her introduction to *Whores and Other Feminists*, writer Jill Nagle addresses the difficult question of how sexualized bodies and subjects might be created anew:

> A central problem for feminists of all stripes, including feminist whores, is opposing the nonconsensual treatment of women as *only* sexual bodies while simultaneously challenging the cultural hierarchies that devalue and stigmatize sexual bodies. To come at it from the other side, how do we value our sexuality when 'to be valued for our sexuality' is a primary instrument of our oppression?[89]

Millar provides a possible answer to Nagle's question in suggesting a performance model of sex as an alternative to those that position sexuality as an object of exchange. Sex is not a ticket that women have and men try to get; it is, rather, a "creative process of building something from a set of available elements."[90] Sex is a collaboration similar to two or more musicians engaged in the production of music, he contends. Problematic valuations of celibacy are undermined insofar as people do not own music or sex prior to its creation. Devaluations of so-called sluts are also rendered nonsensical, he continues, since the musician and lover become better with practice. Furthermore, because collaboration is premised upon "affirmative participation," Millar's conceptualization of sex works against discursive and experiential ambiguities and ambivalences that blur the boundaries between sex and assault.[91] Although it is debatable whether Millar's model is applicable to discussions of sex work (musicians are, after all, often paid for their skills), when sex is conceived as a cooperative performance, it can no longer be viewed as prone to scarcity (a characterization that otherwise certainly strengthens the market for selling sexual services). As surmised by sex-positive feminist Carol Queen, "I'd be glad to see sex work wither away because everyone became so sex-positive that a market for our services no longer existed."[92]

It is my position that shifting discourse is more effective than resisting repression. Sex-positive feminism buys into the repressive hypothesis, but as Foucault reminds us, Western society has not been predicated on the repression of sexuality. Rather, Western society "speaks verbosely of its own silence, takes great pains to relate in detail the things it does not say [and] denounces the powers it exercises."[93] Ignoring this argument, particularly when framing sex workers as outlaws, sex-positive feminism inadvertently overlooks the content of what is being liberated. Not only does this situation reproduce established discourses, insofar as discourses aimed at stemming repression allow for the proliferation of those that circulate in repression's silence, but it also runs the risk of foreclosing the production of alternatively sexualized bodies and subjects. Butler explains that foreclosure "works not to prohibit existing desire but to produce certain kinds of objects and to bar others from the field of social production."[94] Here, we shift the discussion from oppositional celebrations of deviance to processes of normalization, namely how power operates in the privileging of certain sexualities, gender constructions, and labour practices as well as how it is productive of counter-narratives that simultaneously create and limit possibilities.

But the relationship between signification and normative discourse and politics is not linear. Although the bonds between sex work and biological specificity through desire indicate that sex work reifies sexual difference, this claim is complicated by psychoanalytic theory. Desire and fantasy, as psychically constructed relations to internal and external objects, are signifying processes subject to condensations, reversals, and displacements. In this way, there is no clear-cut linearity between fantasy and the object of desire. But fantasy, for Cowie, does not constitute an unlimited array of possibilities that bear no connection to the social within which it arises. One needs to be able to access the fantasy scenario in order for the fantasy or identification to work for the subject. It is the unconscious, revealed in the compulsion to repeat, that disables any full mastery over this process and further complicates the status of choice. Returning to the question of repression, we might ask whether, in its attempt to liberate sex and sexuality, sex-positive feminism enacts textual repressions of its own – a silencing of the complex interplay between politics and the psyche that can operate to destabilize the free choice upon which it depends.

But we all have blind spots when it comes to feminist theory and analyses of the politics of sexuality. This situation has to do with the fact that we develop what I have been calling affective attachments both to the practices we analyze and to the frameworks we use to analyze. Because pornography and sex work are practices that are dependent on affect for their successful constitution, the affective intensity of the terrain is intensified, which, in turn, complicates the relationships we develop to these objects of analysis. Regarding feminist frameworks used to understand pornography and sex work, attachments to these frameworks are formed through processes of identification insofar as attachment implies that identification has already taken place. And it is through this close relationship to identification that attachment sometimes becomes a means of negotiating shame in feminist theorizations of pornography and sex work.

Paranoid Witness and Reparative Disengagement
Reading Feminist Writings on Heterosexuality

4

In order to investigate the affective dimensions of feminist theory and the complicated attachments thinkers develop to feminist arguments and frameworks of analysis more closely, I use Eve Kosofsky Sedgwick's analysis in "Paranoid Reading and Reparative Reading, or You're So Paranoid, You Probably Think This Essay Is about You." Here, she rejects the common focus on whether knowledge is true and instead focuses on how knowledge is performative. She asks, "What does knowledge *do* – the pursuit of it, the having and exposing of it, the receiving again of knowledge of what one already knows? *How,* in short, is knowledge performative, and how best does one move among its causes and effects?"[1] The variable causes and effects of knowledge can be political when considering the production of social actors or the legitimization of institutions and discourses. They can also be psychoanalytic; encountering knowledge, whether it is accepted or rejected, is always of psychic significance.

Sedgwick examines the psychoanalytic qualities of knowledge through an application of Melanie Klein's work on the paranoid-schizoid (paranoid) position and the reparative-depressive (reparative) position to a study of academic reading and writing practices.[2] Turning away from Freudian drive theory, the study of object relations focuses on how the psyche is shaped by its relationships to various (and often variable) objects. Sedgwick describes Klein's paranoid position as one that is riddled with terrible "hatred, envy, and anxiety."[3] That is because, when in the paranoid position, subjects relate to the part-object, thereby splitting objects and experiences into those that are wholly good and those that are wholly bad.[4] Here, there is a heightened awareness of the perceived dangers posed by the world around them. "By contrast, the depressive [or reparative] position is an anxiety-mitigating achievement that the infant or adult only sometimes, and often only briefly, succeeds in inhabiting."[5] This position enables subjects to use their own resources to "assemble or 'repair' the murderous part-objects into something like a whole" – a whole that can then become a more satisfying object of identification.[6] The reparative position is marked by ambivalence in that subjects simultaneously perceive both the good and bad qualities of the object.

As opposed to developmental stages, pathologies, structures, or "diagnostic personality types," the paranoid and reparative positions are relational.[7] "The term 'position' describes the characteristic posture that the ego takes up with respect to its objects … [Klein] wanted to convey, with the idea of position, a much more flexible to-and-fro process between one and the other."[8] We do not simply work through internal conflict to safely reside on the reparative side of the polarity but constantly move back and forth between the two. As Sedgwick clarifies, the paranoid and reparative positions might be thought of as practices – practices of relating to objects, including our theoretical relation to objects, to different theories, and even to theory itself as an object.

In order to study the question of how radical and sex-positive feminist texts "do," I draw on Sedgwick's appropriation of Klein's work on paranoid and reparative reading and writing practices. But I do not just ask how radical and sex-positive feminisms do as sites for political knowledge; I also ask how they do psychoanalytically through the theoretical frameworks they employ and the politics they profess. Radical feminism, for example, does a good job of bearing witness to heterosexual violence, but it is also prone to residing within the paranoid position. In contrast, sex-positive feminism tends toward the reparative position. This position too has its limitations, as it often falls into "manic-reparation" when questions of gender inequality are evaded or when theorists focus on positive affect alone. These dynamics are mirrored in the manner in which radical and sex-positive feminisms narrate past, present, and future in their conceptualizations of the subject. I conclude that texts that neither dismiss nor remain stuck within historical injury are perhaps most substantively reparative.

Bearing Witness to Gendered Violence

One of the ways that radical feminist texts "do" psychoanalytically is by bearing witness to gendered violence. This function is particularly important in cases of trauma. According to psychoanalyst and socialist feminist Juliet Mitchell, "Trauma ... create[s] a breach in a protective covering of such severity that it cannot be coped with by the usual mechanisms by which we deal with pain or loss. The severity of the breach is such that even if the incident is expected, the experience cannot be foretold."[9]

Trauma is thus an extreme injury whose severity cannot be known before the fact. Psychoanalytic literary theorist Cathy Caruth also links trauma to injury and knowledge. She borrows Sigmund Freud's suggestion that trauma occupies the space between knowing and not knowing. In being unable to integrate or assimilate into the ego as the ego was previously constituted, trauma recedes from language and deliberation only to reemerge in one's life through unconscious reenactment.[10] Repetition, therefore, becomes the "attempt to tell us of a reality ... that is not otherwise available."[11] When the telling of trauma becomes deliberate, for Mitchell, it stops being an experiential bedrock for damaged psychic states. Or as articulated by Sharon Rosenberg, trauma requires a witness so that it does not continue as a nonclosure of an event that repeats itself in the present.[12] When situated in language, the event is enclosed, and thus psychically contained, within the boundaries of a clear beginning and end. Here, the subject's internal "thou" is reconstituted.[13] But the subject is not the same as "the person who existed prior to the trauma ... that person [is] irretrievably, and regrettably, lost."[14] Rather, Ann J. Cahill explains, a new self emerges, integrating the significance of the traumatic experience without allowing it to dominate the subject's person.

Processes of testimony and witness work against repression.[15] As explained by Ruth Stein, how one relates to the emotional resonance of repressed memories is central to the process of making them conscious. "In repression, what is lacking is not consciousness – or at least effects in consciousness of a repressed content, or representation – but self-relatedness, ownership, responsiveness to feedback that would lead to experiencing the meaning of the behaviour."[16] It is affect that we dissociate from, that we refuse to experience as "belonging to the self."[17] Similarly, Shoshana Felman explains the unconscious as a kind of "unmeant knowledge which escapes intentionality and *meaning*"; it is that "which the subject cannot recognize, assume as his, *appropriate*."[18] For Stein, as well as for Freud, lifting repression thus requires making repressed content *self*-conscious by remembering the *meaning* of the memory through incorporating the repressed content as "part of the 'I.'"[19] Here, one's affective perception must match how one thinks of the memory. Affect plays a crucial role in the process of making repressed content conscious – it serves as a point of access to thoughts that might otherwise remain unknown.

Radical feminist writings can be theorized as bearing witness to gendered violence. Rather than providing a unique and distinct other who might listen to an individual woman's testimony, radical feminism provides a testimony of its own. It both recognizes and vocalizes potentially traumatic forms of experience to begin the process of working through and to provide an opening for victims to reconstitute the internal thou. For example, Andrea Dworkin stresses the urgency for male solidarity in the fight to end sexual assault:

> Every three minutes a woman is being raped. Every eighteen seconds a woman is being beaten. There is nothing abstract about it. It is happening right now as I am speaking ... We women. We don't have forever. Some of us don't have another week or another day to take time for you to discuss whatever it is that will enable you to go out into those streets and do something. We are very close to death. All women are.[20]

Although Dworkin's prose might be read as inflammatory, this focus on injury serves an affective purpose. Because repression operates through a dissociation of thought from emotion, lifting repression requires that they be associated again. In this way, we might argue that radical feminists like Dworkin do a good job of bearing witness to gendered violence precisely because their writing tends to be so emotionally charged and sensational. For Rosenberg, "to witness can be understood as a summoning of one to listen to another's remembrance."[21] If we are to take this task seriously, listening may involve listening not just to the content of another's remembrance but also to the affective resonance of that remembrance. Here, we evoke the idea of the affective witness. The witness, like the traumatized, must not just understand the testimony intellectually but must feel it as well.

By focusing on systemic forms of oppression and their affective resonance, the radical feminist affective witness becomes effective in the face of insidious trauma. Feminist therapist Laura S. Brown expands traditional understandings of trauma in her piece "Not Outside the Range." Sources of trauma include everyday forms of systemic oppression, small, accumulated offences over time, and common threats to personal integrity and safety.[22] Such trauma can spread through constructed social groups targeted for particular kinds of violence, she explains. One does not have to be gay-bashed, sexually assaulted, or subjected to racist hate crimes to experience trauma; the mere existence and threat of such violence can be destabilizing enough. This is how Brown arrives at the idea of insidious rape trauma, which can arise on account of living in a society where there is a high prevalence of sexual violence and where even so-called normal sex can sometimes rely on assault scripts. Being attentive to personal constitution and history, however, Brown is aware that what might be traumatic for one individual will not be for another. "The same event will not always be traumatic for different people," Mitchell agrees, even though the experience might be similar "whoever the sufferer."[23] In this way, although it is certainly not the case that most women experience insidious rape trauma in their lifetimes, it is fair to assume that the existence of sexual assault will negatively affect some women's subjective sense of personal security and that some will find this lack of security traumatizing.

Radical feminism does an effective job of bearing witness to this insidious trauma, particularly writings focused on heterosexual romance and sex. Dworkin's view of love would no doubt be resonant not just for survivors of domestic violence but also for heterosexual women who may have experienced subtle forms of abuse stemming from gendered inequities in relationships. She writes that romantic love, within the patriarchal imaginary, is founded on a "mythic celebration of female negation."[24] "For a woman, love is defined as her willingness to submit to her own annihilation" through a sacrifice of her identity and bodily integrity.[25] Similarly, Catharine MacKinnon's bleak view of heterosexuality might ring true for women whose accumulated experiences of heterosexual sex have been mediated primarily through the discourse of intercourse-as-violation.[26] That some feminists find Dworkin and MacKinnon healing whereas others find their work infuriating need not be only an expression of political and theoretical investments. Because knowledge "does," as Sedgwick argues, one's reception of the feminist text is shaped by how it reflects one's personal experiences as well as by how one relates to those experiences emotionally. In this way, an attraction to radical feminist writings might be on account of a reader's emotional needs and a rejection might be due to a reader engaging in psychic defence.

Radical Feminist Paranoid Reading and Writing Practices
Although radical feminism does a good job of bearing witness to gendered violence and insidious trauma, it draws heavily on paranoid reading and writing practices.[27] Its reliance upon the part-object is particularly evident. Here, internal objects are crystallized as either all good or all bad and are projected back onto external objects as an ego-defence mechanism that ostensibly minimizes fear and distress, albeit ineffectively.[28] In *Intercourse*, for example, Dworkin renders men, the penis, and intercourse as objects that are all bad. Doing so helps to protect the radical feminist ego by externalizing masculinity and its discontents (aggression, violence, and sexual self-centredness) onto something outside the self (men and patriarchy), which enables the self to remain pure (in this case, feminine and/or feminist).

Closely related is paranoia's goal of minimizing negative affect, Sedgwick explains. In line with Silvan Tomkins, she writes that a "strategy of anticipatory negative affect can have ... the effect of entirely blocking the potentially operative goal of seeking positive affect."[29] In striving so hard to avoid or put an end to the negative emotions that arise through the exercise of sexist meanings used to organize heterosexual practice, Dworkin has completely eclipsed searching for more affirming ways women might be sexual with men, nor does she spend much time looking at queer alternatives. In this way, she forecloses the goal of seeking positive affect. For Dworkin, it is "inconceivable to imagine joy as a guarantor of truth."[30]

Sedgwick further argues that paranoia is anticipatory in its imperative to avoid any and all bad surprises. It is a future-oriented positionality that scurries backward and forward.[31] "Because there must be no bad surprises, and because learning of the possibility of a bad surprise would itself constitute a bad surprise, paranoia requires that bad news be always already known."[32] In her vehement critique of the discourses that lend meaning to heterosexual practice, Dworkin implores caution for those seeking pleasurable heterosexual intercourse. Any pleasure had is a moment stolen from the pervasive discourse of intercourse-as-violation – a discursive threat that must be known in advance to avoid any future surprise. Although the discourses that lend meaning to heterosexual practices are constantly evolving, Dworkin concentrates on the most dire of them all and reads this constellation of historical representations onto representations in the future.

In addition, paranoia is characterized by what Sedgwick terms "knowledge in the form of exposure."[33] Paranoia "acts as though its work would be accomplished if only it could finally, this time, somehow get its story truly known."[34] For Dworkin, and radical feminism more generally, this work is the elimination of patriarchal social relations through exposures of male violence, including unveiling the violence that underlies the history of the modern white, propertied, liberal subject and his supposed universalism. Whereas Dworkin consistently speaks of the discourse of intercourse-as-violation, MacKinnon retells the story of heterosexual sex's situatedness within patriarchal social relations. Of course, these violences are already well known to feminism, but they sometimes remain masked as benevolent or normal in mainstream discourses of heterosexual sex. In this way, continuing to name heterosexual violence operates as a healing process. This emphasis on looking for hidden violence, where "the fundamental category of consciousness is the relation between hidden-shown," can also have its shortcomings.[35] This schema, Sedgwick explains, assumes and requires a certain "naïveté in those who make up the audience for these unveilings."[36] Here, the audience is subordinate to the speaker's masterly knowledge, and other possible modes of inquiry are eclipsed.

Paranoia can further be defined as a humiliation-based "strong theory," Tomkins explains: "A humiliation theory is strong to the extent to which it enables more and more experiences to be accounted for as instances of humiliating experiences."[37] Related to paranoia's anticipatory imperative and emphasis on exposure, strong theories need to continually widen the scope of their surveillance in order to ensure future humiliation is avoided. Here, we are reminded of radical feminism's tendency to view the world through the singular lens of sexism and patriarchy – a singular lens that disallows one to think through other dynamics that might be operative. When we understand the world in a reductive way, our response to its problems tends to be tautological. Essentially, strong theories continue to prove the assumptions they started with over and over again; they scan the world for what they are looking for and amplify it.[38] Sedgwick further explains that strong theories do not become stronger by "obviating or alleviating humiliation" but become "stronger exactly insofar as [they] fail to do so."[39] In this way, they gain strength through their failures to protect subjects from negative affect.[40] Thus Tomkins concludes that "affect theory must be effective to be weak."[41] When effective, we are moved out of the paranoid position and the fear of humiliation that this position entails. This movement is exactly what we do not see in Dworkin. Her need to theorize the discourse of intercourse-as-violation becomes increasingly pressing with every analysis.[42]

As a strong theory that relates to the part-object through an anticipatory emphasis on knowledge in the form of exposure, radical feminism's focus on violence against women only amplifies the negative affect it attempts to mitigate by overlooking ambiguity, complexity, and contradiction. It would seem, then, in contradiction to our previous discussion of the radical feminist affective witness, that radical feminism is not able to do the reparative labour needed to move readers toward a more healing relation to the world; radical feminism leaves readers immobilized within the bad news they have received. When read through Freud's distinction between mourning and melancholia, we might argue that reparation falls in line with the work of mourning. It necessitates an ability to recognize both the good and bad aspects of the object – a confusion that can help encourage the subject to repair external objects "as representatives of those inside that are damaged."[43] Once the restored object is internalized, the subject can begin the work of letting go of what has been lost to move forward. Paranoia, conversely, tends toward melancholia in that it remains stuck within loss as a "condition of uncompleted grief."[44] Here, for Judith Butler, we encounter the limit of the subject's reflexivity because one cannot reflect upon the loss one has experienced. "Unowned and incomplete, melancholia is the limit to the subject's sense of pouvoir, its sense of what it can accomplish and, in that sense, its power."[45] The same is true of feminist theories. Like Butler's argument that heterosexuality is based on melancholic identification through the loss of homosexual attachment, the work of Dworkin and MacKinnon might involve a melancholic loss of egalitarian heterosexuality. Radical feminism's direct address of systemic oppression and gendered social relations cannot guarantee political transformation but, instead, endlessly rehashes sexually injurious histories without ever moving outside their conceptual logic. In this way, loss, like radical feminism's tendency toward strong theory, ensnares the theorist in a need for repetition – a passionate attachment formed through an absence of resolution.

We find that the psychoanalytic orientation of feminist texts affects our complex thinking and feeling responses to them. Reading and writing styles certainly shape how we respond to texts even though the reader's response can never be determined in advance. Here, we again revisit Sedgwick's focus on what texts "do." In the case of radical feminism, a paranoid positionality stuck in melancholia becomes the limit of what it is able to accomplish. In bearing witness to heterosexual and gendered violence, it runs the risk of retraumatizing survivors.[46] This outcome is partially due to radical feminism's modernist orientation, no doubt. Dworkin argues that she has identified a discourse (the discourse of intercourse-as-violation) that has the effect of truth. Although we understand the difference between an effect of truth and "Truth," this ambiguity becomes obscure without an explicit use of poststructural tools. As a result, radical feminism's identification of heterosexual intercourse's discursive organization can be read as declaring a certainty – one that may be healing for some, as an affirmation of experience, and terrifying for others, as a promise of experiences yet to come. Recalling the work of Brown, we can argue, then, that Dworkin's text *Intercourse* suffers from insidious rape trauma while risking insidious rape trauma in its readership. Arising on account of the text's situatedness within the paranoid position, this circumstance strengthens the reader's passionate attachments to the text either as disavowal or as a means of working through insidious rape trauma via a continuous exposure to the potential risks associated with heterosexual intercourse.

Sex-Positive Feminism, Reparation, and Manic-Reparation

There are, however, many theorists who use reparative reading and writing strategies in thinking about sex and sexuality. Ann Cvetkovich's reading of butch-femme relations, for instance, offers a nuanced analysis that provides anxiety-mitigating alternatives. Unlike MacKinnon's reading of patriarchal heterosexual sex as an act of subordination – "subject verb object" – "being fucked" is read as an "active and eager" desire that does not equate receptivity with passivity.[47] But because heterosexual penetration has a history of constructing the bottom as "humiliated by or used for the pleasure of the person doing the fucking or penetrating," Cvetkovich explains that the applicability of butch-femme relations to heterosexuality is limited.[48] Readings of the "fuckee" as passive and stigmatized might continue to cling to women's bodies as the subjects most often, but not exclusively, entered in heterosexual intercourse. Here, Cvetkovich is able to accept ambivalence without marking the act of being entered as all good or all bad. In this way, fucking, when applied to heterosexual women, no longer need be considered a murderous part-object. The object, being fucked, can be understood as affirmative, with Cvetkovich remaining mindful of the manner in which interpretive fields are shaped by political and economic modes of social organization.

The same reparative potential can be seen in Elizabeth Cowie's reading of desire and fantasy. Because fantasy is marked by condensations, reversals, and displacements, the fantasy scenario, she explains, may not present objects and elements for what they are. As a result, heteronormative pornography need not mean only female sexual availability for male consumption. The traditional image of female genital display for male masturbatory pleasure, for example, might also signify for a man "the wish to be found loveable in one's sex."[49] Desire's co-optation to fantasy, however, remains limited as a "textually orchestrated ... set of oppositions" that are still circumscribed by reality and social relations even though not fully determined by them.[50] Lynne Segal puts forward a similar argument in her discussion of pornographic tropes, whereas Thomas Macaulay Millar's performance model of sex offers an alternative to paradigms that constitute female sexuality as an object of exchange. But in stressing the collaborative potentials of sex, he does not forget his purpose: disrupting sexual assault scripts. Millar, Cvetkovich, Cowie, and Segal all repair heterosexual sex by assembling it into a more complex and satisfying *whole* available for identification.

Shannon Bell's recent book *Fast Feminism* can be interpreted as providing an example of theory residing in the reparative position that we have not yet investigated. Offering a "new-old feminism grounded in politics, performance and philosophy," she uses poststructural feminism, queer theory, postfeminism, and speed theory while continuing to draw upon the second-wave feminist demand for sexual and social equality.[51] Bell takes up the longstanding feminist concern of phallic overentitlement. By reading the clitoris, urethra, and vagina (or "CUV") as one integrated sex organ, she lends the fast feminist a *female* phallus as part of her physical and psycho body. "The term 'female phallus' is used to refer to both the fleshy, spongy, biophysical penis equivalent [in terms of erectile tissue and ejaculatory function] and [also] the social right to agency that in the past has only accompanied the male biophysical organ."[52]

The reparative potential of Bell's analysis becomes obvious when compared with Freud's developmental reading of the clitoris as a location of activity that must be renounced in favour of the vagina's passive receptivity for proper female sexual maturity.[53] It is also seen in comparison with

Dworkin's paranoid reading of gendered physiology. For Dworkin, women are defined through their "hole" as a perpetual mark of vulnerability.[54] Here, woman remains stuck in fear of the terrible part-object. Bell, conversely, seems to align woman with Deborah Britzman's position on thinking as "the capacity to find newer and newer ideas that can be unmoored from the frightening qualities of concrete symbolization."[55]

Another example of a reparative reading of sexuality is found in media theorist Kath Albury's article "Reading Porn Reparatively." Here, Albury makes an argument for reparative readings of pornography through the use of Sedgwick and Foucault while actively producing a reparative reading of her own. According to Albury, a problem with the pornography debates of the 1980s and 1990s was that "porn could only ever be 'all good' or 'all bad.'"[56] Not only did this argument orient feminists toward the paranoid position, but these kinds of readings also foreclosed theorists' capacities to teach and learn about "*changing* sexual practices and sexual subjectivities."[57] Even mainstream texts that employ stereotypical gender representations can offer insight into "*how* ... meanings c[o]me into being and change ... over time."[58] "All good" and "all bad" readings also obscure the complicated ways that the same pornographic text might carry different meanings for different subjects, according to Albury. For example, she cites the pornographic film *Hard Love and How to Fuck in High Heels* as a reparative production for its eroticization of "verbal communication and sexual negotiation."[59] It is still the case, however, that some might view the film, and its success outside queer female audiences, as a co-optation of lesbian sex for heterosexual male audiences, Albury explains. When acts of so-called liberation are simultaneously understood to produce new power relations, the need to find perfect representations or to reproduce criticisms that do not tell us anything we do not already know diminishes.[60] Instead, we can accept many contradictory readings as potentially valid – including those that position the reader in the dead end of rejecting everything that does not offer radical social change – while continuing to ask "What else?" of the sexual representations we analyze and consume.[61]

Reparative writing practices are unique in their ability to remain mindful of historical inequities while maintaining hope. "Hope," according to Sedgwick, "is among the energies by which the reparatively positioned reader tries to organize the fragments and part-objects she encounters or creates."[62] "Because the reader [or writer] has room to realize that the future may be different from the present, it is also possible for her to entertain such profoundly ... relieving, ethically crucial possibilities as that the past, in turn, could have happened differently from the way it actually did."[63] But reparative reading practices are not always straightforwardly so; sometimes reparative readings fall into manic-reparation. Although reading and writing practices grounded in manic-reparation insist that the future may be different from the present, this concentration on future possibilities does not properly attend to the relationship that history bears to the present. In addition, manic-reparation's attempt to repair external objects as representations of internally damaged ones operates as a defence mechanism to protect the ego and the objects to which the ego is passionately attached.[64] For the child, this might involve wishing ill upon a parent and then overcompensating with reparative offerings such as gifts to ensure the parent, as an important object, survives.[65] For sex-positive feminism, this is based on the well-intentioned attempt to repair objects that have been damaged by second-wave feminism, including masculinity, femininity, male sexual desire, pornography, sex work, BDSM, certain kinds of queer sex, heterosexual sex, and heterosexuality more generally. This reparative tendency becomes manic when focused on female empowerment and positive affect without any attention to social or economic constraints. In other words, manic-reparation, when applied to the political, engages in a kind of reparative *disengagement* by glossing over what ought not be left unrecognized.

We find a quintessential example of manic-reparation in Eva Pendleton's argument that sex work queers heterosexuality. With the exception of one sentence questioning gendered disparities in sex work, Pendleton's analysis focuses almost exclusively on its positive potential. Her argument that sex work disrupts the "norm of white procreative heterosexuality," that it provides an "indictment of gender roles by demanding payment for playing them," that it reverses the terms under which "men feel entitled to unlimited access to women's bodies," and that it "proliferat[es] sexual deviances" misses the manner in which exchanging sex for material reward has been integral to normative heterosexuality.[66] In the attempt to resignify sex work and curb sex-worker stigmatization, Pendleton's analysis, then, remains ahistorical.

Camille Paglia's theory that date rape does not exist is also inclined toward manic-reparation. She argues that women need to accept the dangers inherent to heterosexual sex and start taking responsibility for their own self-protection.[67] In doing so, Paglia's analysis can be read as empowering in her presupposition that women already possess or could easily acquire the skills needed to protect themselves. But this emphasis on female autonomy and self-sufficiency does not consider the social context within which date rape occurs, including heterosexist readings of female sexuality and sexual assault myths. Taking ownership of one's safety does help to move woman outside the category of victim but only because very real power differentials are erased. As seen, feminist theorists who tend toward the manic-reparative position reject ideas and theories that inscribe women as subject to physical and emotional harm. Whereas a paranoid radical feminism says, "I have been hurt, bear witness to my pain," a manic sex-positive feminism says, "I can't be hurt because I have renarrativized my experiences and gender relations more generally."[68]

Reading and Writing Past, Present, and Future

How do radical and sex-positive feminisms align with paranoid, reparative, and manic-reparative positions? How do feminist narrations of past, present, and future inform the reading and writing practices in which they engage? Radical feminism's conception of the subject, no doubt, is oriented toward the past. This orientation does not contradict my previous reading that it participates in an anticipatory paranoia that scurries backward and forward because radical feminism's future-oriented posture takes the form of reading the past onto the future. Wendy Brown's work on the politicization of historically marginalized subjects provides clarification. She argues that subjects who have experienced oppression on the basis of identity (women, the LGBTQ community, racialized persons, and disabled folk) sometimes become dependent upon narratives of exclusion in order to continue to exist within a politicized form; "insofar as they are premised on exclusion from a universal ideal, politicized identities require that ideal, as well as their exclusion from it, for their own perpetuity as identities."[69] Radical feminism fits this description of wounded attachment in continually referencing histories of exclusion as a means of politicizing the category of woman. These histories, then, are repeatedly highlighted so as to ensure they are not written onto the future, which, of course, inadvertently guarantees that they are.

Just as Sedgwick's positions are about relating to objects through affect, so too is identity politics' relation to historical narratives. Radical feminism's focus on historical exclusion results in an affective orientation toward *ressentiment*. Building on the work of Friedrich Nietzsche, Brown defines *ressentiment* as based on a "moralizing revenge of the powerless."[70] This "slave morality," or "triumph of the weak as weak," means that in addition to an investment in their own subjugation and impotence, historically marginalized subjects become invested in "the satisfactions of revenge that ceaselessly reenact even as they redistribute the injuries of marginalization."[71] By seeking a cause for their suffering and agents in whom they can induce feelings of guilt, Brown explains, the wounded are able to place themselves in a position of moral superiority while constructing themselves as politically innocent. Within this melancholic compulsion to repeat, suffering is fetishized and negative feelings acquire the status of truth.[72]

Brown's description of identity politics as tending toward a *ressentiment* that equates the good with the weak is clearly evident in Dworkin. Here, women are reproduced as an object of injury to enact moral revenge on men, who are located in a position of strength. By externalizing all blame for the conditions of female existence onto men, Dworkin is able to turn "weakness into an accomplishment" and injustice into strength.[73] In dominant discourse, the reproduction of the category of "woman" as a site of subjugation is done so that, like Nietzsche's herd, women might become patient, humble, and obedient. Dworkin uses it, however, to provide women with a morally superior continuity of identity from where to forward political demands. Even if we argue that she does not overtly moralize from a position of disadvantage, it is still the case, according to her logic, that women need to continually retell themselves as marginal in order to hold men accountable for their position of privilege.

Conversely, sex-positive feminism's conception of the subject is future-oriented. Rather than reading the past onto the future, sex-positive feminism imagines a better future and reads it onto the present. Here, the passionate attachment is to pleasure as organized through an affective orientation to omnipotence. We have already noted that sex-positive feminism's exclusive focus on positive affect constitutes a manic relation to the part-object. As queer historian Heather Love eloquently puts it, the "politics of optimism diminishes the suffering of ... [marginalized] historical subjects," but it also "blinds us to the continuities between past and present."[74] Because in mania "survival is located in a phantasy of omnipotence," the reader tries to control the present and future through a disavowal of the past.[75] It is easy to slide into manic-reparation when trying to read and write from the reparative position for any duration of time; omnipotence is seductive, and it must be given up when accepting both the good and bad qualities of the object.[76] Omnipotence can be aligned with master morality, which equates the good with the powerful and substitutes the concept of evil for bad in a supposed affirmation of life.[77]

As informed by their orientations to past, present, and future, radical feminists tend toward paranoia, whereas sex-positive feminists tend toward manic-reparation. Radical feminism fixates on the past and writes it onto the future to continually repeat bad news on a loop. Relating to the part-object and amplifying negative affect only reaffirms the importance of slave morality and its ability to expose the moral failings of those in a position of privilege. Here, women become stuck within an ontology of being that focuses on the "I can" or, as the case may be, the "I cannot."[78] Conversely, sex-positive feminism's fixation on the future and tendency to write it onto the present is premised on a refusal to hear bad news. Here, relating to the part-object occurs through a master morality that recognizes only ontologies of becoming. The subject becomes bound to "the possibilities of the 'I will,'" which, although divorced from the limitations of wounded attachment, remain ungrounded and divorced from history.[79] Both positions, a paranoid attachment to the past and a manic-reparative attachment to the future, might perform productive labour for readers and writers, but I still wonder whether there might be a more reparative means of relating to past, present, and future.[80]

Nietzsche's emphasis on "active forgetfulness," with its supposed promise of "happiness, cheerfulness, hope, pride," is sometimes argued to be an effective means of escaping a transcendent past that ties us to an ontology of being.[81] But this is a manic defence that erases the past's relationship to the present. Sara Ahmed warns of the political dangers of overvaluing happiness in Western liberal democracies. Becoming a British subject, often considered a part of the good life, requires both accepting empire as "the gift of happiness" and forgetting about the violence of colonial rule.[82] Judith/Jack Halberstam argues similarly in discussing Toni Morrison's novel *Beloved*. On the one hand, forgetting about traumatic histories transforms spaces previously filled with heartache into spaces filled with life.[83] Here, forgetting fosters new becomings for those struggling with slavery and its legacies. On the other hand, the novel "reminds us that forgetting can easily be used as a tool of dominant culture to push the past aside in order to maintain the fantasy and fiction of a just and tolerant present."[84] Radical feminism's obsession with remembering is not adequate either. In addition to remaining stuck within an ontology of being, its wounded attachment to injury is conducive to insidious trauma and melancholia. Social transformation thus requires finding new means of narrativizing the relationships between past, present, and future that are neither causally connected nor entirely divorced. Robyn Wiegman gestures toward a solution in her recent article "The Times We're In." Although her intention is to trouble the dualism often reproduced in thinking about the paranoid and reparative positions, her reading of affect and time moves well between past, present, and future. She explains that feminist affect theory's "critical engagement with reparative reading moves in multiple temporal directions, aspiring toward the future as well as the past in affective tonalities that reimagine the project of living in and through the present."[85] Here, the theorist mediates between continuity and discontinuity, between past and future, in a manner that does not remain stuck in either forgetting or remembering. A moderated remembrance becomes a healing praxis when witnessing the past is intimately tied to projects and possibilities for the present and future.[86] And this praxis is reparative, for as Wiegman explains through Sedgwick, "reparation ... [is] about learning how to build small worlds of sustenance that cultivate a different present and future for the [past] that one has suffered."[87]

Conclusion

Radical feminism's ability to bear witness to gendered violence is enabled through an inflammatory mode of address that foregrounds the affective meaning of social relations for readers and writers. But the work of the radical feminist affective witness is inhibited through a paranoid orientation to knowledge – an orientation that does, to use Sedgwick's language, in melancholic ways that can reproduce insidious rape trauma. Related is radical feminism's wounded attachment to narratives of historical marginalization that politicize the category of "woman" while reproducing her as an object of injury. By moving away from a strict focus on the past to possibilities for the future, sex-positive feminism is able to avoid these shortcomings. But, here, the tendency is toward manic-reparation. Sex-positive feminism focuses on positive affect and processes of becoming at the expense of historical inequities. Essentially, the past is divorced from the present as a manic defence against the effects of being stuck within narratives that position gendered subjects in damaging ways. When looking at the different ways that radical and sex-positive feminisms do, we find that it is not the meaning of objects or texts themselves that matters. What matters, as Susanna Paasonen explains, are the effects of objects and texts – how they shape the social in ways that might not have occurred without their existence.[88]

The question becomes, then, how we might bear witness to gendered violence in a manner that neither remains tied to the past nor effaces the past's relationship to the present in holding open possibilities for the future. Asked another way, how do we begin the work of reparation without falling into paranoid or manic reading and writing practices that oscillate between chronic remembering and forgetting? In addition to Wiegman's suggestion of cultivating different presents and futures in relation to difficult pasts, we can look to feminist political theorist Lois McNay's work on routinized oppositional practices. McNay questions the "trope of indeterminacy" wherein a "ceaseless contestation of boundaries" is understood to be the most radical of political practices.[89]

This approach to the subject and lived social reality attends to the manner in which social identities and practices are always mediated and constrained. On the one hand, McNay explains, indeterminacy gives life its open-ended character. On the other, it overlooks the manner in which social life is mediated by "embodied tendencies and social structures [that are] ... relatively predictable and ... routinely contribute to the reproduction of systemic inequalities of race, class and gender."[90] As a result, McNay borrows from legal theorist Davina Cooper to argue that there are ways of moving away from the past that still attend to its legacies. Routinization and entrenchment, they suggest, move outside the opposition between determinacy and indeterminacy. McNay and Cooper focus on the past only to the extent that it can be mobilized to undermine unfavourable historical narratives as they are expressed in the present. This practice, she explains, is "crucial for oppositional practices 'from recycling to lesbian motherhood'" so that they might "gain a wider political currency" and be "less vulnerable to attack from opponents."[91] Encouraging temporary determinacy for presently indeterminate counterhegemonic practices is neither ahistorical nor fixed within historical exclusion.

But the relationships we as thinkers form to past, present, and future cannot be divorced from questions of affect. Radical feminism's focus on the past immerses it in negative affect even while it does everything possible to avoid feeling bad. This is, no doubt, one of the reasons radical feminism is rejected. Feminists too fall prey to the disciplining effects of an anti-feminist culture that would police supposedly improper expressions of emotion in social justice scholarship through "ideologies of style."[92] But although the imperative is either to erase negative affect or to speak about it only in particular ways, negative affect, like positive affect, can be productive. This is particularly the case when we allow negative feelings to coexist with those that are positive, including the reparative energies of hope, in thinking about sustaining ways of surviving the present and co-creating new futures.

Conclusion
Ambivalent Attachments

This book has explored the complex affective relationships readers form to feminist frameworks and arguments, by revisiting the feminist sex wars and the politics of heterosexuality. The feminist sex wars, at least in academic circles, it seems, left sex-positive feminism a historical victor and radical feminism the discarded failure. We find that in mediating between radical feminism's relentless fight against gender inequality and sex-positive feminism's critique of radical feminism, heterosexual practices have no inherent or fixed universal meaning even though they are often deployed as gendered strategies of stratification. This nuanced argument begins the work of bridging generational divides constructed and reinforced by the feminist sex wars. But rather than celebrate radical feminism in a manner that forgets about the lessons learned from sex-positive feminism (or poststructural and queer theory, for that matter), my interest, in the words of Ann Cvetkovich, has been to nurture a "sex positivity that can embrace negativity."[1]

Looking more closely at the complex affective relationships readers form to feminist frameworks and arguments requires reviewing how such attachments are formed in the first place. Attachments to theory can be explained through Judith Butler's writing on subject formation. Subjects develop attachments to discourses that inaugurate them into subjecthood.[2] If we believe theory, like discourse, also has interpellative effects, it is not a stretch to argue that we develop attachments to theory as an investment in the perpetuity of our intellectual and political existence, that we come to identify with theories in the same messy and contradictory ways that characterize all identification.

In part, we develop attachments to feminist arguments and frameworks of analysis on the basis of what we feel they can provide for us. "When we talk about an object of desire" (including desired theories), social affect scholar Lauren Berlant explains, "we are really talking about a cluster of promises."[3] We develop attachments by reason of all those other unnamed benefits that we imagine to be circulating around or in proximity to the object of desire.[4] Part of what clusters around the object, at least if it is academic in character, is what Robyn Wiegman describes as the "field imaginary," which "denotes 'the disciplinary unconscious' – that domain of critical interpellation through which practitioners learn to pursue particular objects, protocols, methods of study, and interpretative vocabularies as the means for expressing and inhabiting their belonging to the field."[5] This is to say that among what clusters around our desired arguments and frameworks are the rules of the disciplines within which they are immersed, whether those rules be conscious or not.

Studying epistemology can help to clarify how at least one aspect of the field imaginary might affect the attachments we form to texts. The epistemological orientation of texts shapes the manner in which we feel recognized by them. As a modernist discourse, radical feminism is concerned with structural power relations. This concern often results in a focus on the commonalities of how women have been socially positioned *as women*. Turning toward the radical feminist text, then, might be premised upon a desire to feel socially recognized on the basis of one's lived specificity. To be seen as who we "are," vis-à-vis how we have been socially named by discourse, can operate as an affirmation of our being and our capacities to act in the world, including our capacities to potentially undermine how identity categories shape our social existence. But insofar as the category of woman is always already a kind of misrecognition, recognizing this lived specificity paradoxically demands *misrecognition* from the radical feminist text. The tendencies of radical feminist practices of textual recognition come into focus when compared with poststructural modes of address. There are those for whom contingency, intersectionality, and fragmentation might be the only reprieve from the injuries of misrecognition. Because, as just suggested, textual recognition is a practice of *mis*recognition, one that potentially limits the breadth of our being, these readers turn toward texts that refuse to witness any universality of identity-based experience. But whether we are discussing misrecognition in the interests of recognition (a turn to the radical feminist text) or misrecognition as an avoidance of misrecognition (a turn to the poststructural feminist text), how texts participate in the production of intellectual politicized subjectivity always affects our reception of them. This ongoing production of intellectual subjectivity shifts in contradictory ways insofar as we are continually transformed through our encounters with feminist texts. And because we, as individuals, are always known differently, even in confrontation with similar bodies of literature, no one particular feminism can ever do justice to every feminist subject.

Regardless of the motivations that bring us to attach to particular objects, it is often very difficult for attachments to shift. Indeed, as Berlant quotes Sigmund Freud, "people never willingly abandon a libidinal position, not even, indeed, when a substitute is already beckoning them."[6] I hypothesize that radical feminism is so frequently rejected partly on account of the intimate relationships we form to competing feminist arguments and frameworks of analysis. Because we form narcissistic attachments to the specificity of our own social existence, rejections of radical feminism may sometimes have to do with the intimate connections and identifications readers form to feminisms that argue against or seem incongruent with this modernist politic. We strive toward stability in our libidinal positions and, as a result, reject ideas that force a reorganization of our political self-perception. A turn toward the radical feminist text, even a nuanced or skeptical turn, could compromise our current attachments by positioning us as indirectly sympathetic to essentialist or anti-sex sentiment given how radical feminism is popularly received. And because learning always involves a reorganization of the psyche, the risks involved with letting in theories deemed incongruent with the self are too high. In this way, we may prefer to reject radical feminism outright rather than compromise our political and theoretical agency as premised on an adherence to coherent methodological frameworks.

But what about the question of *ambivalent* attachments? How is it possible to be attracted to the cutting certainty of radical feminism while formally adhering to a poststructural feminist framework of analysis? How can we feel vindicated by radical feminism's sexual politics, particularly its critique of heterosexuality and heterosexual practices, while acknowledging the political utility of sex-positive feminist argumentation? And most basic, how is it possible to develop emotional investments in seemingly oppositional political and theoretical feminist frameworks?

Although I am not going to provide definitive answers here, I put forward a suggestion that could be used in future theorizing. For Butler, understanding subjection requires that we refuse to posit dualisms between the political and the psychic.[7] That is because an apparently voluntary turn to the interpellative hail already assumes that we recognize ourselves in line with its dictates. In other words, a psychoanalytic reading of interpellation anticipates a consciousness already formed by power; interpellation "presupposes not only that the inculcation of conscience already has taken place, but that conscience, understood as the psychic operation of a regulatory norm, constitutes a specifically psychic and social working of power on which interpellation depends but for which it can give no account."[8] If figured through Freud's early metaphor of the onion skin for the conscious-unconscious mind, the formation of conscience along specific discursive lines may already always be deferred to a previous moment that is not so much temporal as it is spatial, lying in deeper and deeper layers of the subject's (un)consciousness. Here, the inculcation of social being might not be conscious but unconscious – an internalization of regulatory norms without the subject's full awareness.

Because it is always partially unconscious, the inculcation of social being is also never linear nor complete. As expressed by Jacqueline Rose, "the concepts of fantasy and the unconscious rule any notion of pure imposition or full acquisition [of identity] out of bounds."[9] Put another way, the unconscious, with its unstructured irrationality, renders impossible a psyche fully constituted by power. For Rose, this situation is particularly evident when it comes to the internalization of gendered identity: "because there is no continuity of psychic life, so there is not stability of sexual identity, no position for women (or for men) which is ever simply achieved."[10] As a result, our lives are lived as an endless and repeated failure of identity.[11] Passionate attachments to theory arise on account of psychoanalytic processes similar to those at play in subject formation, and since subject formation is never complete, I argue, we develop contradictory investments in the confused particularities of our intellectual existence. The conflicting wishes that occupy the unconscious mind complicate the tangled attachments we form to feminist arguments and frameworks of analysis. If the subject, consciously or not, understands itself to be constituted through theory and if the subject is at its core contradictory, we ought not be surprised that we develop ambivalent attachments to the feminist materials we consume and employ.

I conclude my treatment of ambivalent attachments by returning to Eve Kosofsky Sedgwick's discussion of paranoid and reparative reading and writing practices. Ambivalent attachments to feminist arguments and frameworks are not a paranoid inclination but may, in fact, represent the opposite. That is because opposites do not exist when it comes to paranoia and reparation. Wiegman provides clarification in a recent special issue of *Feminist Theory*. Refusing to posit a dualism between the two, she explains that "both the paranoid and the reparative positions are responses to the same environmental conditions of ambivalence."[12] Indeed, feminist theorist Clare Hemmings picks up the conversation to describe experiences of paranoia and reparation as "co-extensive."[13] It is not to the critical theorist's benefit to see them otherwise; when we focus on reparation alone, we risk overlooking structural dynamics that enable inequalities to persist.[14] But as the case may be, Melanie Klein never intended the reparative position to be read one-dimensionally. Theorists sometimes wrongheadedly use the reparative position, feminist film theorist Jackie Stacey explains, as a means of wishing away ambivalence. Because the reparative position relates to the whole object, it accepts both the good and bad qualities of the object and is therefore itself an ambivalent inclination; "Klein's model of reparation is thus always and necessarily one based upon a conflicted object relation and never one in which love operates free of hate."[15] As a result, ambivalent and conflicting attachments, including those that are marked by contradictory positive and negative emotions, might indicate that we have momentarily achieved a more mature (and reparative) relation to feminist arguments and frameworks of analysis.

Rather than solving my dilemma concerning ambivalent attachments, this book has made me feel more comfortable with them. My sympathies for radical feminism, notably its cutting criticism of heterosexuality, can coexist with an assertion that sex-positive feminism is often right in its criticisms of radical feminist wrongs. These sympathies are able to coexist with the poststructural queer orientation I take in my theorizing. My conviction is that ambivalence can be a productive place from which to begin thinking. If I had taken a paranoid or manic-reparative approach to radical feminism, this book would never have been written. Feminist knowledges do not just "do" singularly; they often do in conflict as they collide and produce new contradictions. It is my hope that you felt as ambivalent reading this text as I did writing it.

Notes

Introduction

1 This discarding of radical feminism could comprise what Clare Hemmings calls a progress narrative. Here, the history of feminist thought is believed to have followed a trajectory from "sameness to difference, singularity to multiplicity, or simplicity to complexity." Clare Hemmings, *Why Stories Matter: The Political Grammar of Feminism Theory* (Durham, NC: Duke University Press, 2011), 36. According to this framing, radical feminism had to be left behind as anachronistic, as out of time with current political and theoretical concerns. My revisiting of radical feminism in this text could be further interpreted through Hemmings as a return narrative wherein the politics of earlier feminisms are synthesized with lessons of the third wave.

2 This curious personal history can be explained through Shoshana Felman's position that "human discourse can by definition never be entirely in agreement with itself"; we never fully have complete knowledge of what we say or do. Shoshana Felman, "Psychoanalysis and Education: Teaching Terminable and Interminable," in *Learning Desire: Perspectives on Pedagogy, Culture, and the Unsaid*, ed. Sharon Todd (New York: Routledge, 1997), 24.

3 The continued utility of radical feminism is affirmed by Allyson Mitchell in describing the process whereby previously unpoliticized students become feminist in her women's studies classrooms. She notes that it is not uncommon for students to first adopt a radical feminist position. Although this politics eventually becomes more sophisticated, the initial persuasiveness of radical and lesbian feminisms indicates their continued relevance as both political and pedagogical tools. See Chelsey Lichtman, "Deeply Lez: Allyson Mitchell," interview, *Trade* 5 (2004): 23.

Barbara A. Crow also provides a defence of radical feminism in arguing that it is largely responsible for affording contemporary feminists the cushion of freedoms they currently enjoy. Barbara A. Crow, "Introduction: Radical Feminism," in *Radical Feminism: A Documentary Reader*, ed. Barbara A. Crow (New York: New York University Press, 2000), 1.

4 This investment is in line with Ann Cvetkovich's suggestion of using a "reparative perspective that embraces conflict rather than separating out right from wrong." Ann Cvetkovich, *Depression: A Public Feeling* (Durham, NC: Duke University Press, 2012), 10.

5 Kathy Miriam also defends radical feminist argumentation on heterosexuality. She provides a phenomenological account of poet and essayist Adrienne Rich's position on the "law of male sex-right" and the "connection between heteronormativity and male supremacy." Kathy Miriam, "Toward a Phenomenology of Sex-Right: Reviving Radical Feminist Theory of Compulsory Heterosexuality," *Hypatia* 22, 1 (2007): 211–12. In doing so, she lends credence to Catharine MacKinnon's understanding of the social meanings of heterosexual practices in patriarchal societies and to Carole Pateman's critique of how liberalism structures gendered experiences of dominance and subordination. See Catharine MacKinnon, *Toward a Feminist Theory of the State* (Cambridge, MA: Harvard University Press, 1989), and Carol Pateman, "The Fraternal Social Contract" (1980) in *Contemporary Political Philosophy: An Anthology*, 2nd ed., ed. Robert E. Goodin and Philip Pettit (Oxford: Blackwell Publishers, 2006).

6 Louis Althusser, "Ideology and Ideological State Apparatuses" (1970), in *Mapping Ideology*, ed. Slavoj Žižek (New York: Verso, 1995), 123.

7 Jane Flax, "The End of Innocence," in *Feminists Theorize the Political*, ed. Judith Butler and Joan W. Scott (New York: Routledge, 1992), 447. Flax discusses the function this kind of "innocent" knowledge serves in the constructed opposition between power and "true" knowledge in Western Enlightenment thinking.

8 Stuart Hall, "Subjects in History" (1997), in *The House That Race Built*, ed. Wahneema Lubiano (New York: Vintage Books, 1998), 289.

9 Michel Foucault, *Discipline and Punish: The Birth of the Prison*, trans. Alan Sheridan (1977; reprint, New York: Vintage Books, 1995), 27.

10 Judith Butler, *The Psychic Life of Power: Theories in Subjection* (Stanford, CA: Stanford University Press, 1997), 1–2.

11 Ibid., 15.

12 Judith Butler, *Gender Trouble: Feminism and the Subversion of Identity* (1990; reprint, New York: Routledge, 2006), 1.

13 See Judith Butler, "Contingent Foundations," in *Feminists Theorize the Political*, ed. Judith Butler and Joan W. Scott, 3–21 (New York: Routledge, 1992); and Judith Butler, "Subjects of Sex/Gender/Desire," in *Gender Trouble: Feminism and the Subversion of Identity*, 1–46 (1990; reprint, New York: Routledge, 2006).

14 See Nancy C.M. Hartsock, "Foucault on Power: A Theory for Women?" in *Feminism/Postmodernism*, ed. Linda J. Nicholson, 157–75 (New York: Routledge, 1990); and Nancy C.M. Hartsock, *The Feminist Standpoint Revisited and Other Essays* (Boulder, CO: Westview, 1998).
15 Political economist Meg Luxton concurs, arguing that women still face sexist discrimination *as women* (personal communication with author, 2012).
16 Sigmund Freud, cited in Natalie Loveless, "Practice in the Flesh of Theory: Art, Research, and the Fine Arts PhD," *Canadian Journal of Communication* 37, 1 (2012): 95.
17 Shoshana Felman, cited in Deborah P. Britzman, *After-Education: Anna Freud, Melanie Klein, and Psychoanalytic Histories of Learning* (Albany: State University of New York Press, 2003), 133.
18 Loveless, "Practice in the Flesh," 95.
19 Robyn Wiegman, *Object Lessons* (Durham, NC: Duke University Press, 2012), 8.
20 Ibid., 20.
21 Britzman, *After-Education*, 125.
22 Ibid., 126.
23 Judith Butler, "Gender Is Burning: Questions of Appropriation and Subversion" (1993), in *The Visual Culture Reader*, ed. Nicholas Mirzoeff (New York: Routledge, 1999), 448–49.
24 Butler, *Psychic Life of Power*, 28.
25 Ibid., 112–13, 7.
26 For instance, radical feminist texts tend to produce women as morally superior victims, whereas sex-positive feminist texts seem to produce women as active sexual agents. Feminist texts that are poststructural in orientation can sometimes position readers as either included or excluded from their dense academic prose.
27 Cvetkovich, *Depression*, 4. Some theorists write affect as "precognitive sensory experience" and emotion as the "cultural constructs and conscious processes that emerge from them." Ibid. Cvetkovich, conversely, allows affect, emotion, and feeling to touch upon and bleed into one another.
28 Sara Ahmed, *The Cultural Politics of Emotion* (New York: Routledge, 2004). This understanding is in opposition to biological or psychological views of emotion.
29 This is the case whether, for instance, we are responding to the anger of radical feminism or to sex-positive feminism's emphasis on pleasure.
30 Susanna Paasonen, "Strange Bedfellows: Pornography, Affect and Feminist Reading," *Feminist Theory* 8, 1 (2007): 46.
31 Ruth Stein, *Psychoanalytic Theories of Affect* (New York: Praeger, 1991), 177.
32 Britzman, *After-Education*, 126.
33 Ibid.
34 Both radical and socialist feminisms are concerned with structural power relations, but whereas socialist feminism concentrates on capitalism, class, and exploitations

of female labour, radical feminism concentrates on patriarchy, gender, and exploitations of female sexuality. Similarities between some sex-positive and poststructural feminisms can be found in their view that sexual practices have no singular meaning. Here, the difference is that poststructural feminism arrives at this position on the basis of epistemological premises, whereas sex-positive feminism is motivated by its political purpose.

35 Robyn Wiegman, "The Times We're In: Queer Feminist Criticism and the Reparative 'Turn,'" *Feminist Theory* 15, 1 (2014): 5.
36 Sharon Rosenberg, "Neither Forgotten nor Fully Remembered: Tracing an Ambivalent Public Memory on the 10th Anniversary of the Montreal Massacre," *Feminist Theory* 4, 1 (2003): 10.
37 Catharine MacKinnon, "Feminism, Marxism, Method, and the State: An Agenda for Theory" (1982), in *Feminist Social Thought: A Reader*, ed. Diana Tietjens Meyers (New York: Routledge, 1997), 66. As MacKinnon argues, "sexuality is to feminism what work is to marxism: that which is most one's own, yet most taken away." Ibid., 65.
38 Ibid., 75.
39 Ibid., 73, original emphasis.
40 Andrea Dworkin, "I Want a Twenty-Four-Hour Truce" (1984), in *Transforming a Rape Culture*, rev. ed., ed. Emilie Buchwald, Pamela Fletcher, and Martha Roth (Minneapolis, MN: Milkweed, 2005), 17.
41 This argument is reproduced in many of MacKinnon's books, including *Feminism Unmodified: Discourses on Life and Law* (Cambridge, MA: Harvard University Press, 1987); *Toward a Feminist Theory of the State* (Cambridge, MA: Harvard University Press, 1989); *Only Words* (Cambridge, MA: Harvard University Press, 1993); *Women's Lives, Men's Laws* (Cambridge, MA: Belknap, 2005); and *Are Women Human? And Other International Dialogues* (Cambridge, MA: Belknap, 2006).
42 Dworkin, "I Want a Twenty-Four-Hour Truce," 14–15.
43 Susan Brownmiller, *Against Our Will: Men, Women and Rape* (1975; reprint, New York: Open Road Media, 2013).
44 Most radical feminists remain critical of BDSM (bondage and discipline, dominance and submission, sadism and masochism). Christine Stark, for example, argues that even *feminist* BDSM is a "disturbing and pathetic expression of internalized misogyny." Christine Stark, "Girls to Boyz: Sex Radical Women Promoting Pornography and Prostitution," in *Not for Sale: Feminists Resisting Prostitution and Pornography*, ed. Christine Stark and Rebecca Whisnant (North Melbourne: Spinifex, 2004), 289.
45 One of the reasons it is difficult to identify a sex-positive theory of sexual assault is that sex-positive feminism often uses strategies of discursive reversal. As evident with pornography and sex work, what the radical feminist sees as "bad," the sex-positive feminist sees as "good." This strategy falls short in discussions of sexual assault. Brenda Cossman, personal communication with author, 2012.

46 Camille Paglia, *Sex, Art, and American Culture: Essays* (New York: Vintage Books, 1992), 69. As Paglia asserts, Susan Jacoby calls her "anti-feminist" in a review of Paglia's work in *Newsday*. Ibid., 55, 59.
47 Ibid., 53, 51, 67. Similarly, Katie Roiphe argues against using the term "date rape" when a woman is under the influence. Adult women, she contends, must take responsibility for their own decisions regarding drug and alcohol use. "The idea that only an explicit yes means yes proposes that, like children, women have trouble communicating what they want." Katie Roiphe, "Date Rape's Other Victim," *New York Times*, June 13, 1993, http://www.nytimes.com/1993/06/13/magazine/date-rape-s-other-victim.html.
48 See Jaclyn Friedman and Jessica Valenti, eds., *Yes Means Yes: Visions of Female Sexual Power and a World without Rape* (Berkeley, CA: Seal), 2008. Unlike Paglia and Roiphe, both of whom draw clear distinctions between sex and assault, the authors anthologized in *Yes Means Yes* take a sex-positive continuum approach.
49 Andrea Dworkin, *Intercourse* (1987; reprint, New York: Free Press, 1997).
50 Andrea Dworkin, *Pornography: Men Possessing Women* (New York: Perigee Books, 1981), 69.
51 MacKinnon, "Feminism, Marxism," 75.
52 Catharine MacKinnon, cited in Nina Philadelphoff-Puren, "The Mark of Refusal: Sexual Violence and the Politics of Recontextualization," *Feminist Theory* 5, 3 (2004): 244.
53 Gail Dines, "Unmasking the Pornography Industry" (2003), in *Transforming a Rape Culture*, rev. ed., ed. Emilie Buchwald, Pamela Fletcher, and Martha Roth (Minneapolis, MN: Milkweed, 2005), 107, 113.
54 Robin Morgan, "Theory and Practice: Pornography and Rape," in *Going Too Far: The Personal Chronicle of a Feminist* (New York: Vintage Books, 1978), 169. That is why, for Dines, opposition to violence against women necessitates opposition to pornography. Dines, "Unmasking the Pornography Industry," 114. Contrary to sex-positive feminism, Dines concludes that legitimization will not save the pornography industry by making it more safe and dignified for women. It must be abolished "if we are to take women's lives seriously." Ibid., 107.
55 MacKinnon, "Feminism, Marxism," 76.
56 Kate Millett, quoted in Deborah Brock, "Victim, Nuisance, Fallen Woman, Outlaw, Worker? Making the Identity 'Prostitute' in Canadian Criminal Law," in *Law as a Gendering Practice*, ed. Dorothy E. Chunn and Dany Lacombe (Don Mills, ON: Oxford University Press, 2000), 90. In rebuttal, one might argue it is true that the prostitute sells self-degradation but only within a culture of misogyny where sex workers are stigmatized and where heterosexual intercourse itself becomes a mark of inferiority for those penetrated.
57 Ibid.
58 Sheila Jeffreys, *The Idea of Prostitution* (North Melbourne: Spinifex, 1997), 3, 5.

59 Ibid., 3. In Christine Stark and Rebecca Whisnant, eds., *Not for Sale: Feminists Resisting Prostitution and Pornography* (North Melbourne: Spinifex, 2004), most of the writers use the language of "prostituted" persons and "prostitution survivors" to highlight the patriarchal power dynamics they see as inherent to sex work.

60 Dany Lacombe, *Blue Politics: Pornography and the Law in the Age of Feminism* (Toronto: University of Toronto Press, 1994), 8. Lacombe, herself, identifies as an anti-censorship feminist.

61 Ibid., 7. Shannon Bell makes this argument for what she terms "nonrecuperable queer socialist pornography." Shannon Bell, "Post-porn\Post-anti-porn: Queer Socialist Pornography," in *New Socialisms: Futures beyond Globalization*, ed. Robert Albritton, Shannon Bell, John R. Bell, and Richard Westra (New York: Routledge, 2004), 141. And Sharif Mowlabocus has focused on the democratizing potentials of user-generated pornographies. Webcams enable amateurs to subvert being positioned as objects to be looked at by providing opportunities for direct audience address. Sharif Mowlabocus, "Porn 2.0? Technology, Social Practice, and the New Online Porn Industry," in *Porn.com: Making Sense of Online Pornography*, ed. Feona Attwood (New York: Peter Lang, 2010), 74, 77.

62 See Brenda Cossman, Shannon Bell, Lise Gotell, and Becki L. Ross, eds., *Bad Attitude/s on Trial: Pornography, Feminism, and the Butler Decision* (Toronto: University of Toronto Press, 1997); and Lacombe, *Blue Politics*.

63 See Lynne Segal, "Does Pornography Cause Violence? The Search for Evidence," in *Dirty Looks: Women, Pornography, Power*, ed. Pamela Church Gibson and Roma Gibson (London: British Film Institute, 1993), 15. Segal is perhaps best categorized as a socialist feminist.

64 For a detailed discussion of the relationship between pornography, fantasy, and reality, see Elizabeth Cowie, "Pornography and Fantasy: Psychoanalytic Perspective," in *Sex Exposed: Sexuality and the Pornography Debate*, ed. Pamela Church Gibson and Roma Gibson, 133–52 (New Brunswick, NJ: Rutgers University Press, 1993).

65 Melissa Petro conducts an ethnographic examination of why women enter sex work. Although financial gain is cited most often, many women also talk of curiosity, excitement, enjoyment, freedom, and control as motivating factors. Melissa Petro, "Selling Sex: Women's Participation in the Sex Industry," in *Sex Work Matters: Exploring Money, Power and Intimacy in the Sex Industry*, ed. Melissa Hope Ditmore, Antonia Levy, and Alys Willman (London: Zed Books, 2010), 156, 157, 161.

66 Maggie's: The Toronto Sex Workers Action Project, "Who We Are," 2011, http://maggiestoronto.ca/about.

67 Shannon Bell, *Reading, Writing, and Rewriting the Prostitute Body* (Bloomington: Indiana University Press, 1994), 1. In her chapters "Rewriting the Prostitute Body" and "Prostitute Performances," Bell examines some of the contradictory ways that sex work and sex workers have been discursively produced and self-authored.

Chapter 1

1. This chapter does not use formal Derridean deconstruction. I use the term "deconstruction" loosely, as it is sometimes deployed in cultural studies, to indicate my intent to unpack social codifications of heterosexual intercourse.
2. Andrea Dworkin, *Intercourse* (1987; reprint, New York: Free Press, 1997), 122.
3. Jennifer Wicke, "Through a Gaze Darkly: Pornography's Academic Market," in *Dirty Looks: Women, Pornography, Power*, ed. Pamela Church Gibson and Roma Gibson (London: British Film Institute, 1993), 78.
4. Fernflores contests philosopher Martha Nussbaum's view that Dworkin's novel *Mercy* is unable to think beyond retributive justice. For Fernflores, Dworkin's intent to speak for those who have been brutalized by male violence does not necessitate, and perhaps even precludes, being merciful to the perpetrators of that violence. Rachel Fernflores, "Merciful Interpretation," *Women's Studies: An Interdisciplinary Journal* 38, 3 (2009): 253–72. Serisier studies how Dworkin positions herself inconsistently as an iconic victim in *Mercy* and as a militant feminist icon in her autobiography *Heartbreak*. Andrea Dworkin, *Mercy* (New York: Four Walls Eight Windows, 1990); Andrea Dworkin, *Heartbreak: The Political Memoir of a Feminist Militant* (New York: Basic Books, 2002); Tayna Serisier, "Who Was Andrea? Writing Oneself as a Feminist Icon," *Women: A Cultural Review* 24, 1 (2013): 26–44.
5. It is not always clear whether the fiction authors that Dworkin cites reproduce the discourse of intercourse-as-violation themselves or whether they do so as specific to the characters they develop.
6. Theodore Van De Velde, quoted in Dworkin, *Intercourse*, 64, original emphasis.
7. William Graham Cole, quoted in ibid., 163.
8. Dworkin, *Intercourse*, 152.
9. "Penetration," in *Webster's New World College Dictionary* (2014), http://www.yourdictionary.com/penetration.
10. Cynthia H. Enloe, *Bananas, Beaches and Bases* (Berkeley: University of California Press, 2000). Robert Jensen also makes links between gender and war. He argues that both heterosexual pornography and the American Gulf War depend upon "rendering human beings less-than-fully-human so they can be hurt – in the case of pornography to provide pleasure for men, and in war to protect the comfort of Americans." Robert Jensen, "Blow Bangs and Cluster Bombs: The Cruelty of Men and Americans," in *Not for Sale: Feminists Resisting Prostitution and Pornography*, ed. Christine Stark and Rebecca Whisnant (North Melbourne: Spinifex, 2004), 31.
11. Leo Bersani, "Is the Rectum a Grave?" *October* 43 (1987): 212.
12. Ibid.
13. Ibid.
14. Ibid.
15. The website Lighthouse Teenies (lighthouseteenseries.com), for example, uses concerning categories to organize content, including "Drunk Teens Fucking" and

"Models Sixteen." The website Gangbang Cocks (gangbangcocks.com) is subtitled "Gangs of Men *Violating* Sluts in *Every Hole*" (original emphasis). The popular website Bang Bus (bangbus.com) features a group of men who invite a young woman into their vehicle and offer her payment for sex, but often before she is paid, she is thrown out, or as the site puts it, "They get in our bus so we get in their holes, and then toss them out!" And a Google search for "'no means yes' and 'xxx,'" conducted February 28, 2012, brought up 59,900 results, although some of these were feminist discussions and blog entries. But the example of pornography is tenuous in that pornography's status as fantasy means that it provides an escape from the very social relations it reflects and reproduces.

16 Josey Vogels, "Vampire Mania: It's All about Sex," *Toronto Metro*, November 17, 2009.
17 Ibid.
18 Stuart Hall, "Subjects in History" (1997), in *The House That Race Built*, ed. Wahneema Lubiano (New York: Vintage Books, 1998), 289.
19 Ibid., 290.
20 Friedrich Nietzsche, *On the Genealogy of Morality: A Polemic* (1887), trans. Carol Diethe, ed. Keith Ansell-Pearson (New York: Cambridge University Press, 1997), 28.
21 Judith Butler, "Performative Acts and Gender Constitution" (1988), in *The Feminism and Visual Culture Reader*, ed. Amelie Jones (New York: Routledge, 2003), 394, 402.
22 Ibid., 394.
23 Hall, "Subjects in History," 290, original emphasis.
24 Ibid.
25 Judith Butler, "Gender Is Burning: Questions of Appropriation and Subversion" (1993), in *The Visual Culture Reader*, ed. Nicholas Mirzoeff (New York: Routledge, 1999), 8.
26 Dworkin, *Intercourse*, 122, 123.
27 Ibid., 123. In comparing the penis to a knife, Dworkin makes the same totalizing assertions when speaking of male anatomy. Ibid., 190. But she also speaks of male vulnerability. It is remarkable, Dworkin comments, that men are not the ones who are considered overpowered in intercourse insofar as they are buried inside the body of another; "his penis is surrounded by strong muscles that ... push hard on the tender thing, always so vulnerable no matter how hard." Ibid., 64.
28 Ibid., 122. We can think of Dworkin's reading of gendered anatomy as an identification of a problematic discourse in need of drastic overhaul, just as I have interpreted her reading of heterosexual intercourse more generally. The phrase "*defined by how she is made*" indicates that she is speaking of a representational strategy. Ibid., 122, 123, emphasis added.
29 An example might include women fucking men. This usage, it seems, has only come into linguistic circulation recently.

30 This is, of course, also the case for same-sex desire.
31 Judith Butler, *Gender Trouble: Feminism and the Subversion of Identity* (1990; reprint, New York: Routledge, 2006), 17.
32 Dworkin, *Intercourse*, 97–98, original emphasis.
33 Ibid., 142.
34 Ibid., 123. Here, we find how practices of desire can so easily be aligned with the discourse of intercourse-as-violation. Because heterosexuality is premised on a desire for sexual difference within a political context of inequality, Dworkin argues that women ought to be the deciding partner in sexual interactions with men. She cites politician and suffrage activist Victoria Woodhull's position that women have a "*natural* right" – one that arises out of the act of intercourse itself – "to be entirely self-determining, the controlling and dominating partner, the one whose desire determine[s] the event, the one who both initiates and is the final authority on what the sex is and will be." Ibid., 135, original emphasis.
35 As a result, the propagation of such desiring norms – either as a social value or as an object of critique – can produce intense emotional reactions that are as personal as they are political.
36 Slavoj Žižek, *The Sublime Object of Ideology* (New York: Verso, 1989).
37 Sigmund Freud, cited in Bersani, "Is the Rectum a Grave?" 217.
38 Ibid.
39 Ibid.
40 Ann Cvetkovich, *An Archive of Feelings: Trauma, Sexuality, and Lesbian Public Cultures* (London: Duke University Press, 2003), 51.
41 Ibid., 50.
42 Bersani, "Is the Rectum a Grave?" 218.
43 That is why, Bersani contends, both "women and gay men spread their legs with an unquenchable appetite for destruction." Ibid., 211.
44 Ibid. Shannon Bell resignifies male and female genitalia by making visible the female phallus. This approach has implications for the gendered psychic dynamics discussed by Bersani in unifying the vagina with the clitoris and urethra as an integrated and active sex organ.
45 Judith Butler, *Bodies that Matter: On the Discursive Limits of "Sex"* (New York: Routledge, 1993), x.
46 Ibid., 5.
47 Ibid., 28, 10. The italicization of "matters" is borrowed from Butler's question "Does anything *matter* in or for poststructuralism?" Ibid., 28.
48 On this point, Bersani writes, "The social structures from which it is said that the eroticizing of mastery and subordination derive are … themselves derivations (and sublimations) of the indissociable nature of sexual pleasure and the exercise of the loss of power." Bersani, "Is the Rectum a Grave?" 216.
49 This take is rather different from most feminist theory's investment in what Bersani calls the "redemptive reinvention of sex." Ibid., 215. Here, the tacit or

explicit presupposition is that sex, "in its essence," has the potential to be "less disturbing, less socially abrasive, less violent, more respectful of 'personhood' than it has been in a male-dominated, phallocentric culture." Ibid. As noted, Bersani argues that there might be something about sex that is inherently unredeemable.

50 Ibid., 221. In fact, Bersani himself notes similarities between his project and the radical feminism of Dworkin and Catharine MacKinnon. Like Bersani, they remain suspicious of sex. Dworkin and MacKinnon reject the "liberal distinction between violence and sex" in pornography and assault. Ibid., 214, 215. Instead, they define as "violent the power relation that they see inscribed in the sex acts pornography represents." Ibid., 213. Here, their views support not just a criminalization of assault but also a *"criminalization of sex itself until it has been reinvented."* Ibid., 214, original emphasis. In this way, radical feminists share with Bersani a concern with the pastoral project even while they continue to ascribe to it.

51 Ibid., 217, original emphasis. In this way, Bersani explains, the "oppression of women disguises a fearful male response to the seductiveness of an image of sexual powerlessness." Ibid., 221.

52 Cvetkovich, *Archive of Feelings*, 52.

53 Ibid., 59, original emphasis.

54 Ibid., 60.

55 Dworkin, *Intercourse*, 122.

56 Ibid., ix–x.

57 See Michel Foucault, *The History of Sexuality*, vol. 1, *An Introduction*, trans. Robert Hurley (1978; reprint New York: Vintage Books, 1990).

Chapter 2

1 See Susan Brownmiller, *Against Our Will: Men, Women and Rape* (1975; reprint, New York: Open Road Media, 2013). Quoting Brownmiller, Cahill notes serious problems with her understanding that assault lies in "the specifics of the human genitals" as contextualized by social relations in that it "appeal[s] to biology as a politically innocent field of knowledge." Ann J. Cahill, *Rethinking Rape* (Ithaca, NY: Cornell University Press, 2001), 22, 26.

2 Catherine MacKinnon, *Toward a Feminist Theory of the State* (Cambridge, MA: Harvard University Press, 1989), 173.

3 Ruth Stein, *Psychoanalytic Theories of Affect* (New York: Praeger, 1991), 177.

4 Sara Ahmed, *The Cultural Politics of Emotion* (New York: Routledge, 2004), 8–10, 6.

5 Ibid., 6.

6 Nicola Gavey, *Just Sex? The Cultural Scaffolding of Rape* (New York: Routledge, 2005), 136.

7 Here, I am referring to partners who might play with heterosexist representation.

8 Wendy Hollway, cited in Gavey, *Just Sex?* 103.

9 Gavey, *Just Sex?* 141.

10 Ibid., 106. Gavey is referring to the idea that the sexual liberation movement was amenable to patriarchal capitalism. This is not to argue that it was without benefit, but, as Gavey references writer and activist Beatrix Campbell, it also carried decreased responsibility of men for pregnancy, increased pressures from men for women to be sexual, and an increase in narrowly defined pornographic imagery.
11 Ibid., 139, original emphasis.
12 Ibid., 2.
13 Cahill, *Rethinking Rape*, 38.
14 Here, we see how it might be easy to misread Dworkin and MacKinnon as saying that all heterosexual intercourse is rape. As a result, Cahill contends that our theories of sexual assault ought to acknowledge that "for most women, in most cases, to be raped is a strikingly different experience than to engage in voluntary heterosexual sex." Ibid., 43.
15 Whereas the first scenario could easily align with radical feminist false consciousness arguments, the second borders on anti-feminist in its adherence to common assault myth that women falsely accuse men of "rape." For heterosexual men, the first might involve a refusal to believe he has transgressed another's boundaries when by all legal accounts he has. In the second, he might experience difficulties being intimate with women for fear he will inadvertently wield sex as a weapon.
16 Ahmed, *Cultural Politics of Emotion*, 8.
17 Ibid.
18 Ibid.
19 Camille Paglia, *Sex, Art, and American Culture: Essays* (New York: Vintage Books, 1992), 52, 62, 67. Here, Paglia reverses the feminist position that sexual assault stems from sexist socialization. For her, socialization is women's greatest defence against assault – protection from the state of nature. Despite this claim, she asserts that she is not a biological determinist.
20 Ibid., 51.
21 Specifically, Paglia calls for defensive dating.
22 Cahill, *Rethinking Rape*, 27.
23 Ibid. Or as articulated by Cahill, "it *matters* that sexuality is the medium of the power and violence that are imposed on the victim ... [and] that in the context of the assault, the rapist is sexually aroused." Ibid., original emphasis.
24 This is very much in contrast to the contemporary SlutWalk, a protest movement that squarely places the burden of responsibility on rapists.
25 When women are understood as disproportionately subject to acquaintance assault, a serious social problem receives political representation. As a result, however, women are written as vulnerable to sexual violence. Paradoxically, to the extent that feminist theories do an adequate job of situating their analyses historically, the risk of reproducing women as objects of injury only increases. For instance, Nicola Gavey is mindful of the social, political, and economic contexts

that enable date rape to occur, a contextual mapping that blurs the lines between heterosexual sex and assault while promulgating heterosexual sex as potentially violent.
26 Kevin Bonnycastle, "Rape Uncodified: Reconsidering Bill C-49 Amendments to Canadian Sexual Assault Laws," in *Law as a Gendering Practice*, ed. Dorothy E. Chunn and Dany Lacombe (Don Mills, ON: Oxford University Press, 2000), 61.
27 Bill C-49, quoted in ibid., 73, emphasis added.
28 Bonnycastle, "Rape Uncodified," 73.
29 Ibid., 70.
30 Ibid., 69–70.
31 Dorothy Smith, cited in ibid., 76.
32 Bonnycastle, "Rape Uncodified," 63–64. Bonnycastle's solution is to leave consent and sexual assault uncodified so as to ensure our legal remedies do not congeal the very social problems we are trying to dissipate. Ibid., 76–77. Although he may be correct, the codification of consent in law simultaneously offers protection against rape myths that judges, lawyers, and juries might be prone to fall back upon without informed feminist guidelines.
33 Sharon Marcus, "Fighting Bodies, Fighting Words: A Theory and Politics of Rape Prevention," in *Feminists Theorize the Political*, ed. Judith Butler and Joan W. Scott (New York: Routledge, 1992), 391. This is to say that assault is made possible through cultural narratives that shape not only how assault is performed but also how actors are understood in its enactment. Here, Marcus creates space for women to intervene in assault scripts, thereby intervening in their construction as rapeable. Ibid., 392, 396–97. Ten years later, postcolonial theorist Carine M. Mardorossian contested Marcus's position. She contends that the argument that assault scripts are reproduced in part through women's noncombative response to threats of violence falls into what Michel Foucault critiques as "technologies of the self" in that it holds women responsible for failing to properly reinvent themselves. Carine M. Mardorossian, "Towards a New Feminist Theory of Rape," *Signs: Journal of Women in Culture and Society* 27, 3 (2002): 750, 754.
34 Marcus, "Fighting Bodies," 390.
35 Ahmed, *Cultural Politics of Emotion*, 2.
36 Ibid., 2–3.
37 Gavey, *Just Sex?* 160.
38 Ahmed, *Cultural Politics of Emotion*, 172. More specifically, Ahmed refers to these groups as places for "the transformation of pain into collectivity and resistance." Ibid.
39 Robert Jensen, *Getting Off: Pornography and the End of Masculinity* (Cambridge, MA: South End, 2007), 14.
40 Taylor Lee, "In and Out: A Survivor's Memoir of Stripping," in *Not for Sale: Feminists Resisting Prostitution and Pornography*, ed. Christine Stark and Rebecca Whisnant,

56–63 (North Melbourne: Spinifex, 2004); Chong Kim, "Nobody's Concubine," in Stark and Whisnant, *Not for Sale*, 102–5; Samantha Emery, with Christine Stark, "The Journey Home: An Interview," in Stark and Whisnant, *Not for Sale*, 131–36; Ann Simonton and Carol Smith, "Who Are Women in Pornography? A Conversation," in Stark and Whisnant, *Not for Sale*, 352–61. Catharine MacKinnon also cites childhood sexual abuse as a motivating factor for women entering sex work in her more recent article "Gender – The Future," *Constellations* 17, 4 (2010): 505.

41 Susanna Paasonen, "Strange Bedfellows: Pornography, Affect and Feminist Reading," *Feminist Theory* 8, 1 (2007): 48.
42 Ibid., 47.
43 Ibid.
44 Marcy Sheiner, "Odyssey of a Feminist Pornographer," in *Whores and Other Feminists*, ed. Jill Nagle (New York: Routledge, 1997), 37.
45 Elizabeth Bernstein, *Temporarily Yours: Intimacy, Authenticity, and the Commerce of Sex* (Chicago: University of Chicago Press, 2007).
46 Paasonen, "Strange Bedfellows," 55.
47 Ibid.
48 Ann Cvetkovich, cited in Eve Kosofsky Sedgwick, *Touching Feeling: Affect, Pedagogy, Performativity* (Durham, NC: Duke University Press, 2003), 109. Cvetkovich continues that "the construction of affect as natural might well be part of the discursive apparatus that performs the work of what Foucault has described as the disciplining of the body." Quoted in ibid.
49 Alastair Woods, "Feeling the Political: Trauma and Affect in Contemporary Liberal Capitalism" (Undergraduate thesis, York University, 2011).
50 Peter M. Tiersma, "The Language of Consent in Rape Law," in *The Language of Sexual Crime*, ed. Janet Cotterill (New York: Palgrave Macmillan, 2007), 90, 88, 89. The first example is my own, and the second two belong to Tiersma. Although all three establish the benefits of consent, Tiersma notes that consent still does little to shift the "focus of inquiry from the conduct of the victim to the conduct of the perpetrator," a common problem in many assault trials. Ibid., 90.
51 Sedgwick, *Touching Feeling*, 111.
52 Silvan Tomkins, cited in ibid., 106, original emphasis.
53 Sedgwick, *Touching Feeling*, 114.
54 Silvan Tomkins, quoted in ibid., 99.
55 Ahmed, *Cultural Politics of Emotion*, 5.
56 Ibid., 6.
57 Gavey, *Just Sex?* 139.
58 Catharine MacKinnon, "Feminism, Marxism, Method, and the State: An Agenda for Theory" (1982), in *Feminist Social Thought: A Reader*, ed. Diana Tietjens Meyers (New York: Routledge, 1997), 72.
59 Wendy Brown, cited in Bonnycastle, "Rape Uncodified," 74.

60 *Oxford English Dictionary*, 2011, s.v. "consent," emphasis added, http://www.oed.com/.
61 *Canadian Oxford Dictionary*, 1st ed., s.v. "consensus," "consent."
62 *Oxford English Dictionary*, 2011, s.v. "consensus," http://www.oed.com/.
63 *Dictionary.com*, 2011, s.v. "consensus," http://www.dictionary.com/browse/consensus.
64 *Oxford English Dictionary*, 2011, s.v. "consensus," http://www.oed.com/.
65 Ahmed, *Cultural Politics of Emotion*, 8.
66 Ibid., 4.
67 Paasonen, "Strange Bedfellows," 47.
68 Cahill, *Rethinking Rape*, 7.
69 Ibid., 8, 115, 132.
70 Ibid., 132.
71 For more sex-positive readings on affirmative consent, see Jaclyn Friedman and Jessica Valenti, eds., *Yes Means Yes: Visions of Female Sexual Power and a World without Rape* (Berkeley, CA: Seal, 2008).

Chapter 3
1 Catharine MacKinnon, "Gender – The Future," *Constellations* 17, 4 (2010): 504.
2 Catharine MacKinnon, "Feminism, Marxism, Method, and the State: An Agenda for Theory," in *Feminist Social Thought: A Reader*, ed. Diana Tietjens Meyers (New York: Routledge, 1997), 76.
3 Annie Sprinkle, quoted in the Good for Her Feminist Porn Awards, "What Are the Feminist Porn Awards?" 2015, http://www.feministpornawards.com/what-are-the-feminist-porn-awards.
4 Maggie's: The Toronto Sex Workers Action Project, "Who We Are," 2011, http://maggiestoronto.ca/about.
5 Much of this now-popular discourse relies on the centring of sex-worker knowledge and experience on political discourse. "Nothing about us, without us is for us!" is the slogan upon which Maggie's activism pivots. Ibid.
6 Bill C-36, the Protection of Communities and Exploited Persons Act, became law on December 6, 2014. In addition to criminalizing the purchase of sexual services, the bill makes it illegal to live off the avails of sex work unless in a "legitimate" living arrangement and illegal to knowingly advertise sexual services for financial gain. The actual selling of sexual services, however, remains legal.
7 Dany Lacombe, *Blue Politics: Pornography and the Law in the Age of Feminism* (Toronto: University of Toronto Press, 1994), 43.
8 Gayle Rubin, "Thinking Sex," in *Pleasure and Danger: Exploring Female Sexuality*, ed. Carole S. Vance (Boston: Routledge and Keegan Paul, 1984), 279. In the middle of this pyramid, Rubin places unmarried, heterosexual, monogamous couples; other heterosexuals; masturbators; monogamous, queer couples; and, at the very bottom of the pyramid, she places those practising intergenerational sex. Ibid.

9 Priscilla Alexander, "Feminism, Sex Workers, and Human Rights," in *Whores and Other Feminists*, ed. Jill Nagle (New York: Routledge, 1997), 92.
10 Jill Nagle, "First Ladies of Feminist Porn: A Conversation with Candida Royalle and Debi Sundahl," in Nagle, *Whores and Other Feminists*, 161.
11 Veronica Monet, "No Girls Allowed at the Mustang Ranch," in Nagle, *Whores and Other Feminists*, 218.
12 Susie Bright, "The Prime of Miss Kitty MacKinnon," *Susie Bright's Journal*, 1993, 13, http://susiebright.blogs.com/Old_Static_Site_Files/Prime_Of_Kitty_MacKinnon.pdf.
13 In opposition to the tendency of many sex-positive feminists to frame sex as repressed and sex workers as outlaws, the worker paradigm starts from the premise that sex work is not fundamentally different from other forms of labour mediated by varying degrees of gendered, racialized, and classed forms of exploitation. Approaching it as labour, the argument goes, provides the social legitimacy needed to ameliorate working conditions and further sidesteps damaging empowerment-victimization dichotomies. See Emily van der Meulen, "Canadian and International Policies on Prostitution: Labour Legitimacy, Social Change, and Decriminalization," in *Public Policy for Women: The State, Income Security, and Labour Market Issues*, ed. Marjorie Griffin Cohen and Jane Pulkingham (Toronto: University of Toronto Press, 2009), 347.
14 Here, Foucault contradicts Sigmund Freud's argument that some renunciation of libidinal instinct is necessary for the functioning of civilization and Herbert Marcuse's contention that repression needs to be contextualized within the specificity of its economic and political context. For Marcuse, it is capitalism that has compromised our sexual happiness by subordinating sex to the work imperative. See Herbert Marcuse, *Eros and Civilization: A Philosophical Inquiry into Freud* (1955; reprint, Boston: Beacon, 1966); and Sigmund Freud, *Civilization and Its Discontents*, trans. James Strachey (1961; reprint, New York: W.W. Norton, 1989).
15 Michel Foucault, cited in Eve Kosofsky Sedgwick, *Touching Feeling: Affect, Pedagogy, Performativity* (Durham, NC: Duke University Press, 2003), 9–10.
16 Michel Foucault, *The History of Sexuality*, vol. 1, *An Introduction*, trans. Robert Hurley (1978; reprint, New York: Vintage Books, 1990), 5.
17 Ibid., 12. Foucault is less interested in showing the repressive hypothesis to be false than he is in putting it back within a general economy of discourses on sex and sexuality. Ibid., 11.
18 Ibid., 34.
19 Ibid., 18, 33, 34. The institutional apparatuses for producing knowledge about sex were religious, scientific, technical, medical, political, economic, criminological, administrative, pedagogical, psychiatric, and psychoanalytic, to name a handful.
20 Ibid., 32.
21 Ibid., 8–9.

22 Pamela Church Gibson and Roma Gibson, eds., *Dirty Looks: Women, Pornography, Power* (London: British Film Institute, 1993); Shannon Bell, *Whore Carnival* (New York: Autonomedia, 1995); Jill Nagle, ed., *Whores and Other Feminists* (New York: Routledge, 1997); Katrien Jacobs, Marije Janssen, and Matteo Pasquinelli, eds., *C'Lick Me: A Netporn Studies Reader* (Amsterdam: Institute of Network Cultures, 2007), http://www.networkcultures.org/_uploads/24.pdf.

23 Andrea Dworkin, *Women Hating* (New York: E.P. Dutton, 1974); Andrea Dworkin, *Our Blood: Prophecies and Discourses on Sexual Politics* (New York: Harper and Row, 1976); Andrea Dworkin, *Letters from a War Zone* (New York: Lawrence Hill Books, 1993); Andrea Dworkin, *Heartbreak: The Political Memoir of a Feminist Militant* (New York: Basic Books, 2002).

24 In the introduction to their radical feminist anthology *Not for Sale*, Rebecca Whisnant and Christine Stark argue against the framing of anti-pornography and anti-sex-work feminists as sex-negative. This framing, they maintain, overlooks the complexity of these practices and their connection to "male dominance ... racism, imperialism, militarism and global corporate capitalism." Rebecca Whisnant and Christine Stark, "Introduction," in *Not for Sale: Feminists Resisting Prostitution and Pornography*, ed. Christine Stark and Rebecca Whisnant (North Melbourne: Spinifex, 2004), xiv. It is not only sex-positive feminism, however, that employs divisive naming practices. Radical feminists also sometimes call sex-positive feminists anti-feminist for their unwillingness to seriously consider the unequal relations under which sexuality (particularly heterosexual intercourse) continues to be practised.

25 *Merriam-Webster*, 2015, s.v. "transgression," https://www.merriam-webster.com/dictionary/transgression.

26 Of course, there have also been heterosexist radical feminists.

27 See Adrienne Rich, "Compulsory Heterosexuality and Lesbian Existence" (1980), in *Blood, Bread, and Poetry: Selected Prose, 1979–1985*, 23–75 (New York: W.W. Norton, 1986). Andrea Dworkin's work also insinuates that resisting heterosexuality is a kind of transgression; refusing heterosexual intercourse constitutes "a repudiation of the way in which [women are] expected to manifest [their] humanity." Andrea Dworkin, *Intercourse* (1987; reprint, New York: Free Press, 1997), 122.

28 Feminist knowledges tend to stand in opposition to those emanating from religious, scientific, technical, medical, political, economic, criminological, administrative, pedagogical, psychiatric, and psychoanalytic institutional apparatuses.

29 Simon Hardy, "Feminist Iconoclasm and the Problem of Eroticism," *Sexualities* 3, 1 (2000): 79.

30 This function of pornography is concerning because, as political scientist Brian Duff contends, mainstream pornography often makes claims to truth and strives toward authenticity. Brian Duff, "Confession, Sexuality and Pornography as Sacred Language," *Sexualities* 13, 6 (2010): 690.

31 These websites are unique in offering primarily free user-generated content. Members are able to activate their own accounts (and sometimes their own profile

pages) in order to upload videos that tend to fall into one of three categories: commercial clips pirated by home viewers or posted by companies for advertising purposes, amateur works created by users themselves, and sexually explicit clips from other cultural sources such as movies or educational videos.

32 See Feona Attwood, ed., *Porn.com: Making Sense of Online Pornography* (New York: Peter Lang, 2010); Susanna Paasonen, *Carnal Resonance: Affect and Online Pornography* (Cambridge, MA: MIT Press, 2011); and Dennis Waskul, *Net.seXXX: Readings on Sex, Pornography and the Internet* (New York: Peter Lang, 2004).

33 Sharif Mowlabocus, "Porn 2.0? Technology, Social Practice and the New Online Porn Industry," in *Porn.com: Making Sense of Online Pornography*, ed. Feona Attwood (New York: Peter Lang, 2010), 73.

34 Mowlabocus goes on to explain that these labour practices should not be celebrated uncritically. Because of pornography's precarious and piecework nature, workers are still exploited. As a result, the sexual subjectivities that these websites engender continue to remain compatible with the demands of contemporary capitalism. Ibid., 81.

35 Signifiers used by the BDSM community to indicate fantasy roles include fetish gear and named power positions, such as master versus slave and top versus bottom. In the case of pornographic representation, such elements work to signal to the viewer that they are watching a co-created, mutually pleasurable power play, particularly when coupled with postscene actor dialogue.

36 José van Dijck, "Users Like You? Theorizing Agency in User-Generated Content," *Media, Culture and Society* 31, 1 (2009): 41–58.

37 Jill Nagle, ed., *Whores and Other Feminists* (New York: Routledge, 1997), 277.

38 Eva Pendleton, "Love for Sale: Queering Heterosexuality," in *Whores and Other Feminists*, ed. Jill Nagle (New York: Routledge, 1997), 73.

39 Ibid.

40 Ibid., 78, 76.

41 Ibid., 81, 77. Making men pay is subversive because it "reverses the terms under which men feel entitled to unlimited access to women's bodies." Ibid., 79.

42 Ibid., 77, 76, 79, 76, 73.

43 Jane Scoular, "The 'Subject' of Prostitution: Interpreting the Discursive, Symbolic and Material Position of Sex/Work in Feminist Theory," *Feminist Theory* 5, 3 (2004): 248.

44 Thomas Macaulay Millar, "Toward a Performance Model of Sex," in *Yes Means Yes: Visions of Female Sexual Power and a World without Rape*, ed. Jaclyn Friedman and Jessica Valenti (Berkeley, CA: Seal, 2008), 30, 31. For Millar, sex is often framed as having a supply and demand curve.

45 Ibid., 32. The practice of trying to increase the value of one's so-called commodity can be seen in sex-work practices during the Korean War. As shaped by American racism, Korean sex workers often tried to frame themselves as selling services only to white soldiers insofar as sex workers who serviced black soldiers were not able

to fetch the same price on the market. See Katharine Moon, *Sex among Allies: Military Prostitution in U.S.-Korea Relations* (New York: Columbia University Press, 1997), particularly her chapter "U.S.-ROK Security and Civil-Military Relations."
46 Millar, "Toward a Performance Model," 32.
47 The sex-worker movement's demand "to charge for what other women give for free" indicates the extent to which, even within sex-positive feminism, sexuality continues to be framed as property. Frederique Delacoste and Priscilla Alexander, quoted in Scoular, "'Subject' of Prostitution," 247.
48 Millar, "Toward a Performance Model," 36.
49 For Sharon Marcus, that is why it is important to discard feminist discourses that affirm women's ownership of their bodies and sexuality. Sharon Marcus, "Fighting Bodies, Fighting Words: A Theory and Politics of Rape Prevention," in *Feminists Theorize the Political*, ed. Judith Butler and Joan W. Scott (New York: Routledge, 1992), 398–99.
50 Pendleton, "Love for Sale," 79–80; Judith Butler, "Gender Is Burning: Questions of Appropriation and Subversion" (1993), in *The Visual Culture Reader*, ed. Nicholas Mirzoeff (New York: Routledge, 1999), 454.
51 It may be the case that occasionally clients do, in fact, understand that they are paying not only for sexual services but also for their stylized delivery.
52 Pendleton, "Love for Sale," 78.
53 Sherene Razack, for example, argues that when sex work is "romanticized as rebellion and flight from the conditions of white middle-class femininity," its raced and classed dimensions are overlooked. Sherene Razack, "Race, Space, and Prostitution: The Making of the Bourgeois Subject," *Canadian Journal of Women and the Law* 10, 2 (1998): 340. Instead, she proposes a "relational analysis of bodies and spaces." Ibid., 341.
54 Alex Dymock, "Flogging Sexual Transgression: Interrogating the Costs of 'Fifty Shades,'" *Sexualities* 16, 8 (2013): 881. Dymock makes this argument with regard to E.L. James's recent erotic romance novel *Fifty Shades of Grey* (2011). Because representations of BDSM are thought to be inherently transgressive, they incite a proliferation of discourse that operates as a marketing strategy for the books and associated merchandise.
55 Jim Vernon, personal communication with author, 2007.
56 With regard to this point, Bell articulates Rubin's argument that sex work has become a sexual-political identity to a large part through legal persecution that has transformed it from a transitory job to a permanent vocation. Shannon Bell, *Reading, Writing, and Rewriting the Prostitute Body* (Bloomington: Indiana University Press, 1994), 95. But as Deborah Brock contends, positioning sex work as an outlaw or erotic identity ignores its "economic relations ... and leaves it undifferentiated from other consensual sexual practices ... regulated by the state." Deborah Brock, "Victim, Nuisance, Fallen Woman, Outlaw, Worker? Making the Identity 'Prostitute' in Canadian Criminal Law," in *Law as a Gendering Practice*,

ed. Dorothy E. Chunn and Dany Lacombe (Don Mills, ON: Oxford University Press, 2000), 91.
57 Nina Philadelphoff-Puren, "The Mark of Refusal: Sexual Violence and the Politics of Recontextualization," *Feminist Theory* 5, 3 (2004): 246. In reference to hegemonic reading practices, Philadelphoff-Puren suggests "attending to the 'total speech situation'" by reading texts within the contexts that they arise. Ibid., 247. With regard to MacKinnon's inaudible pornographic "no," doing so would involve focusing "feminist efforts on those cultural discourses that enable it to be heard as 'yes.'" Mikhail Bakhtin, cited in ibid., 254.
58 Mikhail Bakhtin, cited in ibid.
59 Elizabeth Cowie, "Pornography and Fantasy: Psychoanalytic Perspectives" (1992), in *Sex Exposed: Sexuality and the Pornography Debate*, ed. Lynne Segal and Mary McIntosh (New Brunswick, NJ: Rutgers University Press, 1993), 136.
60 Ibid., 137.
61 Ibid., 135.
62 Jacqueline Rose, *Sexuality in the Field of Vision* (1986; reprint, New York: Verso, 2005), 227.
63 Cowie, "Pornography and Fantasy," 152.
64 Lynne Segal, "Sweet Sorrows, Painful Pleasures: Pornography and the Perils of Heterosexual Desire," in *Sex Exposed: Sexuality and the Pornography Debate*, ed. Lynne Segal and Mary McIntosh (New Brunswick, NJ: Rutgers University Press, 1993), 68.
65 Ibid. Here, Segal's contention is that by refusing to distinguish between the small, fragile penis and the phallus as a signifier of male sexual power, pornographic tropes actually create, hide, and sustain male sexual anxieties and vulnerabilities. Ibid., 81, 83. They are not the means through which men "*achieve* power over women" but operate as "proof that men *lack* power over women." Ibid., 76, emphasis added.
66 Cowie, "Pornography and Fantasy," 140–41.
67 Ibid., 139. This type of identification further explains why many heterosexual women find such images arousing. Ibid.
68 But it is still the case that sex work presupposes differential levels of desire between sex worker and client. There is otherwise no reason a client might not demand payment from a worker or a worker might not feel obligated to pay a client.
69 The same argument can be made for those of us with flexible object choice in that the particular embodiment of one's partner(s) is rarely extraneous and is often desired on its own terms.
70 Cowie, "Pornography and Fantasy," 141.
71 That is because, as Cowie articulates it, "fantasy is ... a separate realm from reality, but it also exists only in so far as reality circumscribes it." Ibid., 147. An example can be seen in the child's fantasy of the primal scene; the child may read it as the "father's aggressive penetration of the mother, or as the mother's violent appropriation of the father's penis." Ibid., 140. But although perceptions of the mother

as merely passive are disrupted, the primary relation is still to the phallus and to the question of which parent gets to wield it.
72 Kate Millett, cited in Brock, "Victim, Nuisance?" 90.
73 See Margaret Atwood, *The Handmaid's Tale* (Boston: Houghton Mifflin, 1985).
74 The specificity of how such constraint exercises itself on the subject is, however, indeterminable.
75 According to psychoanalytic legal theorist Renata Salecl, fetishizing choice aligns with liberal ideology insofar as it necessitates the appearance of freedom in self-making and does not account for the fact that the subject is never fully the master of the self. Renata Salecl, "Society of Choice," *Differences: A Journal of Feminist Cultural Studies* 20, 1 (2009): 164, 171, 173.
76 Susanna Paasonen, "Disturbing, Fleshy Texts: Close Looking at Pornography," in *Working with Affect in Feminist Readings: Disturbing Differences*, ed. Marianne Liljeström and Susanna Paasonen (Oxford: Routledge, 2010), 69–70.
77 Ibid., 66, 58.
78 Isobel Armstrong, cited in Susanna Paasonen, "Strange Bedfellows: Pornography, Affect and Feminist Reading," *Feminist Theory* 8, 1 (2007): 46.
79 Amelia Jones, *Seeing Differently: A History and Theory of Identification* (Oxford: Routledge, 2012), 170. If identity tends toward visibility and knowability, identification tends toward ambiguity and process, Jones argues. Identification is "intersectional, complex, relational ... never unitary ... fully coherent," or fixed. Ibid., 8.
80 But, of course, because identification is ambiguous, ambivalent, and never fixed, we sometimes have dramatically varied reactions to objects that ostensibly, at least, are difficult to distinguish in any concrete way. In the case of pornography or sex work, we may find that one image or practice is okay whereas a similar image or practice is not.
81 Laura Kipnis, "(Male) Desire and (Female) Disgust: Reading *Hustler*," in *Cultural Studies*, ed. Lawrence Grossberg, Cary Nelson, and Paula Treichler, 373–91 (New York: Routledge, 1992).
82 It is worth noting here that I might be guilty of only exploring my own fantasized relationship to how the reader relates to texts.
83 Sally Munt, *Queer Attachments: The Cultural Politics of Shame* (Surrey, BC: Ashgate, 2008), 5. This description of shame invokes Jean-Paul Sartre's famous position that "hell is – other people!" Jean-Paul Sartre, *No Exit: And Three Other Plays* (1946; reprint, New York: Vintage International, 1989), 45.
84 Male radical feminists similarly engage in distancing activities by trying to divorce themselves from the shame of other men's moral failings.
85 Elspeth Probyn, *Blush: Faces of Shame* (Minneapolis: University of Minnesota Press, 2005).
86 Munt, *Queer Attachments*, 22.
87 Freud, *Civilization and Its Discontents*, 59.

88 In response to Catherine MacKinnon's reading of pornography as hate speech, Judith Butler responds that the sign can break from its social context to take on new significations or social meanings. See Judith Butler, *Excitable Speech: A Politics of the Performative* (New York: Routledge, 1997).
89 Jill Nagle, "Introduction," in *Whores and Other Feminists*, ed. Jill Nagle (New York: Routledge, 1997), 6.
90 Millar, "Toward a Performance Model," 38.
91 Ibid., 40. As Millar explains, "it is fanciful to imagine a circumstance in which enthusiastic participation quickly turns not to regret, but to denial that consent existed at the time." Ibid., 37.
92 Carol Queen, "Sex Radical Politics, Sex-Positive Feminist Thought, and Whore Stigma," in *Whores and Other Feminists*, ed. Jill Nagle (New York: Routledge, 1997), 132.
93 Foucault, *History of Sexuality*, 8–9.
94 Judith Butler, *The Psychic Life of Power: Theories in Subjection* (Stanford, CA: Stanford University Press, 1997), 25.

Chapter 4

1 Eve Kosofsky Sedgwick, *Touching Feeling: Affect, Pedagogy, Performativity* (Durham, NC: Duke University Press, 2003), 124, original emphasis.
2 From here on, I use the term "paranoid" to refer to the paranoid-schizoid position and "reparative" to refer to the reparative-depressive position. The choice of psychiatric diagnoses to classify what are essentially ordinary processes was unfortunate, as explained in Robert Hinshelwood, Susan Robinson, and Oscar Zarate, *Introducing Melanie Klein* (New York: Totem Books, 1998), 90.
3 Sedgwick, *Touching Feeling*, 128.
4 Hinshelwood, Robinson, and Zarate, *Introducing Melanie Klein*, 173.
5 Sedgwick, *Touching Feeling*, 128.
6 Ibid.
7 Ibid. Here, Klein is moving away from Freud's theory of the oral, anal, and genital phases of development.
8 Robert Hinshelwood, quoted in Sedgwick, *Touching Feeling*, 128.
9 Juliet Mitchell, "Trauma, Recognition and the Place of Language," *Diacritics* 28, 4 (1998): 121.
10 Sigmund Freud, cited in Cathy Caruth, *Unclaimed Experience: Trauma, Narrative, and History* (Baltimore, MD: Johns Hopkins University Press, 1996), 4.
11 Ibid.
12 Sharon Rosenberg, "Intersecting Memories: Bearing Witness to the 1989 Massacre of Women in Montreal," *Hypatia* 11, 4 (1996): 121.
13 Dori Laub, "Truth and Testimony: The Process and the Struggle," in *Trauma: Explorations in Memory*, ed. Cathy Caruth (Baltimore, MD: Johns Hopkins University

Press, 1995), 66. Here, Laub is specifically speaking about the traumas of the Shoah. He explains, "the survivors did not only need to survive so that they could tell their stories; they also needed to tell their stories in order to survive." Ibid., 63.

14 Susan Brison, cited in Ann J. Cahill, *Rethinking Rape* (Ithaca, NY: Cornell University Press, 2001), 130–31.
15 Here, I am speaking about psychoanalytic framings of repression, not about framings that conceive repression as an effect of power, as critiqued by Michel Foucault.
16 Ruth Stein, *Psychoanalytic Theories of Affect* (New York: Praeger, 1991), 181.
17 Ibid.
18 Shoshana Felman, "Psychoanalysis and Education: Teaching Terminable and Interminable," in *Learning Desire: Perspectives on Pedagogy, Culture and the Unsaid*, ed. Sharon Todd (New York: Routledge, 1997), 24, emphasis added.
19 Sigmund Freud, quoted in Stein, *Psychoanalytic Theories*, 182.
20 Andrea Dworkin, "I Want a Twenty-Four-Hour Truce" (1984), in *Transforming a Rape Culture*, rev. ed., ed. Emilie Buchwald, Pamela R. Fletcher, and Martha Roth (Minneapolis, MN: Milkweed, 2005), 14. The second part of the quotation precedes the first in the text. Although Dworkin does not specify, I am guessing this is an American statistic from 1983, the same year her speech was originally delivered.
21 Rosenberg, "Intersecting Memories," 123. The witness must be distinguished from the voyeur who passes by without doing the work of trying to understand what the implications of another's testimony might be for one's "own formation and relations to history." Ibid.
22 *Diagnostic and Statistical Manual of Mental Disorders* (1987), cited in Laura S. Brown, "Not Outside the Range: One Feminist Perspective on Psychic Trauma," in *Trauma: Explorations in Memory*, ed. Cathy Caruth (Baltimore, MD: Johns Hopkins University Press, 1995), 105. Although it has since been amended, this 1987 definition of trauma, as quoted by Brown, maintained that "the person has experienced an event that is outside the range of human experience." Ibid., 100. But human experience, Brown argues, has been defined in accordance with the dominant social class – mainly white, able-bodied, Christian, middle-class men. Ibid., 101. When looking beyond this group, we see that many traumas fall well within the range of what constitutes "normal."
23 Mitchell, "Trauma, Recognition," 121.
24 Andrea Dworkin, *Our Blood: Prophecies and Discourses on Sexual Politics* (New York: Harper and Row, 1976), 105.
25 Ibid.
26 Catharine MacKinnon, *Toward a Feminist Theory of the State* (Cambridge, MA: Harvard University Press, 1989), 137. MacKinnon contends that what we call sexuality and sexual pleasure are often the eroticizations of male dominance and control.
27 Sedgwick outlines five characteristics of paranoid reading and writing practices. Here, I will carefully work through a few.

28 Hinshelwood, Robinson, and Zarate, *Introducing Melanie Klein*, 104, 173.
29 Sedgwick, *Touching Feeling*, 136.
30 Ibid., 138.
31 Ibid., 130.
32 Ibid.
33 Ibid., 138.
34 Ibid.
35 Ibid., 125.
36 Ibid., 125, 141, 138.
37 Silvan Tomkins, quoted in Sedgwick, *Touching Feeling*, 134.
38 *Touching Feeling*, 135. The result, for Sedgwick, is that "writers and readers can damagingly misrecognize whether and where real conceptual work is getting done." Ibid., 136.
39 Ibid., 134.
40 Ibid. Related to paranoia as a strong theory is its mimetic character. "Paranoia seems to require being imitated to be understood, and it, in turn, seems to understand only by imitation." Ibid., 131.
41 Silvan Tomkins, cited in ibid., 134.
42 Whereas Dworkin misses how her work can be tautological, many contemporary critics of radical feminism miss how the disdain sparking their inquiry is the very conclusion they continue to draw over and over again.
43 Hinshelwood, Robinson, and Zarate, *Introducing Melanie Klein*, 105.
44 Judith Butler, *The Psychic Life of Power: Theories in Subjection* (Stanford, CA: Stanford University Press, 1997), 23.
45 Ibid.
46 This question was originally raised for me in conversation with my undergraduate friend and colleague Lorraine Hussey. Even if traumatized reactions to radical feminist texts are unusual, these texts do encourage readers to take up a paranoid relation to masculinity and heterosexuality.
47 Catharine MacKinnon, "Feminism, Marxism, Method, and the State: An Agenda for Theory," in *Feminist Social Thought: A Reader*, ed. Diana Tietjens Meyers (New York: Routledge, 1997), 75; Ann Cvetkovich, *An Archive of Feelings: Trauma, Sexuality, and Lesbian Public Cultures* (London: Duke University Press, 2003), 57.
48 Cvetkovich, *Archive of Feelings*, 59.
49 Elizabeth Cowie, "Pornography and Fantasy: Psychoanalytic Perspectives," in *Sex Exposed: Sexuality and the Pornography Debate*, ed. Lynne Segal and Mary McIntosh (New Brunswick, NJ: Rutgers University Press, 1993), 140–41.
50 Ibid., 141, 147.
51 Shannon Bell, *Fast Feminism* (New York: Autonomedia, 2010), back cover, 16. This approach is itself a reparative inclination to borrow what is useful in another author's analysis, even if flawed, instead of focusing exclusively on criticisms. Bell does not reject earlier feminist theories as a means of advancing her own; she

maintains the relationship new feminist contributions bear to those that came before. As argued by Sedgwick, reparation is both "additive and accretive." Sedgwick, *Touching Feeling*, 146.
52 Bell, *Fast Feminism*, 46.
53 See Sigmund Freud, "Three Essays on the Theory of Sexuality," particularly "The Transformations of Puberty," in *The Standard Edition of the Complete Psychological Works of Sigmund Freud*, vol. 7, trans. James Strachey (1953; reprint, London: Vintage Random House, 2001).
54 Andrea Dworkin, *Intercourse* (New York: Free Press, 1987), 122, 123.
55 Deborah P. Britzman, *After-Education: Anna Freud, Melanie Klein, and Psychoanalytic Histories of Learning* (Albany: State University of New York Press, 2003), 130; Sedgwick, *Touching Feeling*, 128.
56 Kath Albury, "Reading Porn Reparatively," *Sexualities* 12, 5 (2009): 648.
57 Ibid., 650, original emphasis.
58 Ibid., 649, 648, original emphasis.
59 Ibid., 649–50.
60 Ibid.
61 Ibid. Another reparative tendency in Albury's analysis is her refusal to position women who act in pornography either as "inherently liberated or empowered" or as "inherently degraded or demeaned." Ibid., 649.
62 Sedgwick, *Touching Feeling*, 146.
63 Ibid.
64 Hinshelwood, Robinson, and Zarate, *Introducing Melanie Klein*, 113. Here, Hinshelwood and colleagues are describing persecutory guilt, but the definition they provide is similar to manic-reparation.
65 Deborah Britzman, personal communication with author, 2004.
66 Eva Pendleton, "Love for Sale: Queering Heterosexuality," in *Whores and Other Feminists*, ed. Jill Nagle (New York: Routledge, 1997), 73, 81, 79, 73, 77. Brian McNair's analysis of the increased sexualization of culture also tends toward manic-reparation. He argues this is a democratizing tendency that makes capitalist societies more inclusive with little concern for how the increased diversity is also heavily commercialized. Brian McNair, *Striptease Culture: Sex, Media and the Democratization of Desire* (New York: Routledge, 2002).
67 Camille Paglia, *Sex, Art, and American Culture: Essays* (New York: Vintage Books, 1992), 57, 67.
68 A poststructural example of manic-reparation can be found in what Sedgwick has termed "anti-essentialist hegemony." Here, theory becomes "coextensive with the claim ... *It's not natural.*" Sedgwick, *Touching Feeling*, 109, original emphasis. For Sedgwick, this is a paranoid inclination because it relates to the part-object in reading essentialism as all bad and it constitutes a strong theory that must continually widen the scope of its surveillance. I contend, conversely, that it is manic because its interest in minimizing negative affects – such as those arising from fixed gender

differentiation as a strategy of stratification – does not block the goal-seeking positive affect. Sedgwick's and my disagreement here indicates the extent to which Klein's positions can overlap or be ambiguous.

69 Wendy Brown, "Injury, Identity, Politics," in *Mapping Multiculturalism*, ed. Avery Gordon and Christopher Newfield (Minneapolis: University of Minnesota Press, 1996), 155.
70 Ibid., 157.
71 Friedrich Nietzsche, quoted in ibid., 160, 158.
72 Laura Berlant, quoted in Lois McNay, "Feminism and Post-identity Politics: The Problem of Agency," *Constellations* 17, 4 (2010): 513.
73 Friedrich Nietzsche, *On the Genealogy of Morality: A Polemic* (1887), trans. Carol Diethe, ed. Keith Ansell-Pearson (New York: Cambridge University Press, 1997), 30.
74 Heather Love, quoted in Robyn Wiegman, "The Times We're In: Queer Feminist Criticism and the Reparative 'Turn,'" *Feminist Theory* 15, 1 (2014): 14.
75 Gail Lewis, "Not by Criticality Alone," *Feminist Theory* 15, 1 (2014): 36. Sex-positive feminism's tendency toward omnipotence can also be seen in its triumphalism vis-à-vis those feminisms it deems anti-sex. As Lewis explains, triumphalism is a "manic defence leading to its own phantasies of omniscience and omnipotence." Ibid.
76 Britzman, *After-Education*, 148. As Britzman explains, "without the illusion of omnipotence, a certain sense of hope also is lost." Ibid. This observation, of course, has important implications for feminism, which is a discourse largely predicated upon hope for a better future.
77 Nietzsche, *On the Genealogy of Morality*, 19.
78 McNay, "Feminism and Post-identity Politics," 515.
79 Ibid., 513.
80 Clare Hemmings suggests that feminists develop attachments to both paranoid and reparative practices on the basis of the work they do for authors. Clare Hemmings, "The Materials of Reparation," *Feminist Theory* 15, 1 (2014): 27.
81 Nietzsche, *On the Genealogy of Morality*, 38.
82 Sara Ahmed, *The Promise of Happiness* (London: Duke University Press, 2010), 131.
83 Judith Halberstam, *The Queer Art of Failure* (Durham, NC: Duke University Press, 2011), 82.
84 Ibid., 82–83.
85 Wiegman, "The Times We're In," 14.
86 The idea of remembrance as praxis was first raised for me in discussion with feminist theorist Kate Bride while presenting an earlier draft of this chapter at the Canadian Women's Studies Association conference in 2011.
87 Ibid., 11.
88 Elizabeth Edwards and Janice Hart, cited in Susanna Paasonen, *Carnal Resonance: Affect and Online Pornography* (Cambridge, MA: MIT Press, 2011), 68.

89 McNay, "Feminism and Post-identity Politics," 512. Here, McNay is questioning the common poststructural and queer assertion that nonidentity is inherently radical. Ibid., 521.
90 Ibid., 517.
91 Davina Cooper, quoted in ibid., 522. The first part of this passage appears after the second in the original text.
92 Barbara Tomlinson, *Feminism and Affect at the Scene of the Argument: Beyond the Trope of the Angry Feminist* (Philadelphia: Temple University Press, 2010), 1–2.

Conclusion

1 Ann Cvetkovich, *An Archive of Feelings: Trauma, Sexuality, and Lesbian Public Cultures* (London: Duke University Press, 2003), 49. Cvetkovich notes in a later book that we need to "depathologize negative feelings." Ann Cvetkovich, *Depression: A Public Feeling* (Durham, NC: Duke University Press, 2012), 2.
2 Judith Butler, *The Psychic Life of Power: Theories in Subjection* (Stanford, CA: Stanford University Press, 1997), 112–13, 7.
3 Lauren Berlant, "Cruel Optimism," *Differences: A Journal of Feminist Cultural Studies* 17, 3 (2006): 20. That is why Berlant holds that "all attachments are optimistic." Ibid.
4 As Berlant writes, "to phrase 'the object of desire' as a cluster of promises is to allow us to encounter what is incoherent or enigmatic in our attachments ... insofar as proximity to the object means proximity to the cluster of things that the object promises." Ibid.
5 Donald E. Pease, cited in Robyn Wiegman, *Object Lessons* (Durham, NC: Duke University Press, 2012), 14. It is worth noting that Wiegman is suspicious of this characterization in that we are seldom ignorant of the structures that occupy our fields of study.
6 Sigmund Freud, quoted in Berlant, "Cruel Optimism," 22. Berlant defines "cruel optimism" as "a relation of attachment to compromised conditions of possibility." Ibid., 21. Here, the presence of an object threatens the subject's welfare even though it is important to a continued sense of being.
7 Butler, *Psychic Life of Power*, 19.
8 Ibid., 5.
9 Jacqueline Rose, *Sexuality in the Field of Vision* (1986; reprint, New York: Verso, 2005), 15–16.
10 Ibid., 90–91.
11 Ibid., 90, 91. "Feminism's affinity with psychoanalysis," Rose argues, "rests ... with this recognition that there is a resistance to identity at the very heart of psychic life." Ibid., 91. But just because discourse does not shape identity in a one-to-one relation does not mean that it has no bearing on identity. According to Rose, it is through identity, namely the question of how individuals come to recognize themselves as gendered subjects and how social institutions become internalized,

that "psychoanalysis enters the political field." Ibid., 5. Here, the psyche and identity might not be determined by social relations, but they are still produced in a complex relation to them.
12 Robyn Wiegman, "The Times We're In: Queer Feminist Criticism and the Reparative 'Turn,'" *Feminist Theory* 15, 1 (2014): 17. Here, Wiegman is picking up on the work of Berlant.
13 Clare Hemmings, "The Materials of Reparation," *Feminist Theory* 15, 1 (2014): 28.
14 Ibid., 29. As Gail Lewis reads Wiegman, suspicion has its place in the face of damaging hegemonic discourses, yet this suspicion must coexist with reparative encounters with objects. Gail Lewis, "Not by Criticality Alone," *Feminist Theory* 15, 1 (2014): 33.
15 Jackie Stacey, "Wishing Away Ambivalence," *Feminist Theory* 15, 1 (2014): 44, 43.

Bibliography

Ahmed, Sara. *The Cultural Politics of Emotion*. New York: Routledge, 2004.
–. *The Promise of Happiness*. London: Duke University Press, 2010.
Albury, Kath. "Reading Porn Reparatively." *Sexualities* 12, 5 (2009): 647–53. https://doi.org/10.1177/1363460709340373.
Alexander, Priscilla. "Feminism, Sex Workers, and Human Rights." In *Whores and Other Feminists*, ed. Jill Nagle, 83–97. New York: Routledge, 1997.
Althusser, Louis. "Ideology and Ideological State Apparatuses." 1970. In *Mapping Ideology*, ed. Slavoj Žižek, 100–40. New York: Verso, 1995.
Attwood, Feona, ed. *Porn.com: Making Sense of Online Pornography*. New York: Peter Lang, 2010.
Atwood, Margaret. *The Handmaid's Tale*. Boston: Houghton Mifflin, 1985.
Bang Bus. bangbus.com.
Barber, Katherine, ed. *The Canadian Oxford Dictionary*. Don Mills, ON: Oxford University Press, 2001.
Bell, Shannon. *Fast Feminism*. New York: Autonomedia, 2010.
–. "Post-porn\Post-anti-porn: Queer Socialist Pornography." In *New Socialisms: Futures beyond Globalization*, ed. Robert Albritton, Shannon Bell, John R. Bell, and Richard Westra, 139–56. New York: Routledge, 2004.
–. *Reading, Writing, and Rewriting the Prostitute Body*. Bloomington: Indiana University Press, 1994.
–. *Whore Carnival*. New York: Autonomedia, 1995.
Berlant, Lauren. "Cruel Optimism." *Differences: A Journal of Feminist Cultural Studies* 17, 3 (2006): 20–36. https://doi.org/10.1215/10407391-2006-009.

Bernstein, Elizabeth. *Temporarily Yours: Intimacy, Authenticity, and the Commerce of Sex.* Chicago: University of Chicago Press, 2007. https://doi.org/10.7208/chicago/9780226044620.001.0001.

Bersani, Leo. "Is the Rectum a Grave?" *October* 43 (1987): 197–222. https://doi.org/10.2307/3397574.

Bonnycastle, Kevin. "Rape Uncodified: Reconsidering Bill C-49 Amendments to Canadian Sexual Assault Laws." In *Law as a Gendering Practice*, ed. Dorothy E. Chunn and Dany Lacombe, 60–78. Don Mills, ON: Oxford University Press, 2000.

Bright, Susie. "The Prime of Miss Kitty MacKinnon." *Susie Bright's Journal*, 1993. http://susiebright.blogs.com/Old_Static_Site_Files/Prime_Of_Kitty_MacKinnon.pdf.

Britzman, Deborah P. *After-Education: Anna Freud, Melanie Klein, and Psychoanalytic Histories of Learning.* Albany: State University of New York Press, 2003.

Brock, Deborah. "Victim, Nuisance, Fallen Woman, Outlaw, Worker? Making the Identity 'Prostitute' in Canadian Criminal Law." In *Law as a Gendering Practice*, ed. Dorothy E. Chunn and Dany Lacombe, 79–99. Don Mills, ON: Oxford University Press, 2000.

Brown, Laura S. "Not Outside the Range: One Feminist Perspective on Psychic Trauma." In *Trauma: Explorations in Memory*, ed. Cathy Caruth, 100–12. Baltimore, MD: Johns Hopkins University Press, 1995.

Brown, Wendy. "Injury, Identity, Politics." In *Mapping Multiculturalism*, ed. Avery Gordon and Christopher Newfield, 149–66. Minneapolis: University of Minnesota Press, 1996.

Brownmiller, Susan. *Against Our Will: Men, Women and Rape.* 1975. Reprint, New York: Open Road Media, 2013.

Butler, Judith. *Bodies that Matter: On the Discursive Limits of "Sex."* New York: Routledge, 1993.

–. "Contingent Foundations." In *Feminists Theorize the Political*, ed. Judith Butler and Joan W. Scott, 3–21. New York: Routledge, 1992.

–. *Excitable Speech: A Politics of the Performative.* New York: Routledge, 1997.

–. "Gender Is Burning: Questions of Appropriation and Subversion." 1993. In *The Visual Culture Reader*, ed. Nicholas Mirzoeff, 448–62. New York: Routledge, 1999.

–. *Gender Trouble: Feminism and the Subversion of Identity.* 1990. Reprint, New York: Routledge, 2006.

–. "Performative Acts and Gender Constitution." 1988. In *The Feminism and Visual Culture Reader*, ed. Amelie Jones, 482–92. New York: Routledge, 2003.

–. *The Psychic Life of Power: Theories in Subjection.* Stanford, CA: Stanford University Press, 1997.

–. "Subjects of Sex/Gender/Desire." In *Gender Trouble: Feminism and the Subversion of Identity*, 1–46. 1990. Reprint, New York: Routledge, 2006.

Cahill, Ann J. *Rethinking Rape.* Ithaca, NY: Cornell University Press, 2001.

Caruth, Cathy. *Unclaimed Experience: Trauma, Narrative, and History.* Baltimore, MD: Johns Hopkins University Press, 1996.

Cossman, Brenda, Shannon Bell, Lise Gotell, and Becki L. Ross, eds. *Bad Attitude/s on Trial: Pornography, Feminism, and the Butler Decision*. Toronto: University of Toronto Press, 1997.

Cowie, Elizabeth. "Pornography and Fantasy: Psychoanalytic Perspective." In *Sex Exposed: Sexuality and the Pornography Debate*, ed. Lynne Segal and Mary McIntosh, 133–52. New Brunswick, NJ: Rutgers University Press, 1993.

Crow, Barbara A. "Introduction: Radical Feminism." In *Radical Feminism: A Documentary Reader*, ed. Barbara A. Crow, 1–9. New York: New York University Press, 2000. https://doi.org/10.1080/09592310008423272.

Cvetkovich, Ann. *An Archive of Feelings: Trauma, Sexuality, and Lesbian Public Cultures*. London: Duke University Press, 2003. https://doi.org/10.1215/9780822384434.

–. *Depression: A Public Feeling*. Durham, NC: Duke University Press, 2012.

Dines, Gail. "Unmasking the Pornography Industry." 2003. In *Transforming a Rape Culture*, rev. ed., ed. Emilie Buchwald, Pamela Fletcher, and Martha Roth, 105–15. Minneapolis, MN: Milkweed, 2005.

Duff, Brian. "Confession, Sexuality and Pornography as Sacred Language." *Sexualities* 13, 6 (2010): 685–98. https://doi.org/10.1177/1363460710384557.

Dworkin, Andrea. *Heartbreak: The Political Memoir of a Feminist Militant*. New York: Basic Books, 2002.

–. "I Want a Twenty-Four-Hour Truce." 1984. In *Transforming a Rape Culture*, rev. ed., ed. Emilie Buchwald, Pamela Fletcher, and Martha Roth, 11–12. Minneapolis, MN: Milkweed, 2005.

–. *Intercourse*. 1987. Reprint, New York: Free Press, 1997.

–. *Letters from a War Zone*. New York: Lawrence Hill Books, 1993.

–. *Mercy*. New York: Four Walls Eight Windows, 1990.

–. *Our Blood: Prophecies and Discourses on Sexual Politics*. New York: Harper and Row, 1976.

–. *Pornography: Men Possessing Women*. New York: Perigee Books, 1981.

–. *Women Hating*. New York: E.P. Dutton, 1974.

Dymock, Alex. "Flogging Sexual Transgression: Interrogating the Costs of 'Fifty Shades.'" *Sexualities* 16, 8 (2013): 880–95. https://doi.org/10.1177/1363460713508884.

Emery, Samantha, with Christine Stark. "The Journey Home: An Interview." In *Not for Sale: Feminists Resisting Prostitution and Pornography*, ed. Christine Stark and Rebecca Whisnant, 131–36. Melbourne: Spinifex, 2004.

Enloe, Cynthia H. *Bananas, Beaches and Bases*. Berkeley: University of California Press, 2000.

Felman, Shoshana. "Psychoanalysis and Education: Teaching Terminable and Interminable." In *Learning Desire: Perspectives on Pedagogy, Culture, and the Unsaid*, ed. Sharon Todd, 17–43. New York: Routledge, 1997.

Fernflores, Rachel. "Merciful Interpretation." *Women's Studies: An Interdisciplinary Journal* 38, 3 (2009): 253–72. https://doi.org/10.1080/00497870902724653.

Flax, Jane. "The End of Innocence." In *Feminists Theorize the Political*, ed. Judith Butler and Joan W. Scott, 445–63. New York: Routledge, 1992.

Foucault, Michel. *Discipline and Punish: The Birth of the Prison*. Trans. Alan Sheridan. 1977. Reprint, New York: Vintage Books, 1995.

–. *The History of Sexuality*. Vol. 1, *An Introduction*. Trans. Robert Hurley. 1978. Reprint, New York: Vintage Books, 1990.

Freud, Sigmund. *Civilization and Its Discontents*. Trans. James Strachey. 1961. Reprint, New York: W.W. Norton, 1989.

–. "Three Essays on the Theory of Sexuality." In *The Standard Edition of the Complete Psychological Works of Sigmund Freud*, vol. 7, trans. James Strachey, 123–245. 1953. Reprint, London: Vintage Random House, 2001.

Friedman, Jaclyn, and Jessica Valenti, eds. *Yes Means Yes: Visions of Female Sexual Power and a World without Rape*. Berkeley, CA: Seal, 2008.

Gangbang Cocks. gangbangcocks.com.

Gavey, Nicola. *Just Sex? The Cultural Scaffolding of Rape*. New York: Routledge, 2005.

Gibson, Pamela Church, and Roma Gibson, eds. *Dirty Looks: Women, Pornography, Power*. London: British Film Institute, 1993.

The Good for Her Feminist Porn Awards. "What Are the Feminist Porn Awards?" 2015. http://www.feministpornawards.com/what-are-the-feminist-porn-awards.

Halberstam, Judith. *The Queer Art of Failure*. Durham, NC: Duke University Press, 2011. https://doi.org/10.1215/9780822394358.

Hall, Stuart. "Subjects in History." 1997. In *The House That Race Built*, ed. Wahneema Lubiano, 289–99. New York: Vintage Books, 1998.

Hardy, Simon. "Feminist Iconoclasm and the Problem of Eroticism." *Sexualities* 3, 1 (2000): 77–96. https://doi.org/10.1177/136346000003001004.

Hartsock, Nancy C.M. *The Feminist Standpoint Revisited and Other Essays*. Boulder, CO: Westview, 1998.

–. "Foucault on Power: A Theory for Women?" In *Feminism/Postmodernism*, ed. Linda J. Nicholson, 157–75. New York: Routledge, 1990.

Hemmings, Clare. "The Materials of Reparation." *Feminist Theory* 15, 1 (2014): 27–30. https://doi.org/10.1177/1464700113513082.

–. *Why Stories Matter: The Political Grammar of Feminism Theory*. Durham, NC: Duke University Press, 2011.

Hinshelwood, Robert, Susan Robinson, and Oscar Zarate. *Introducing Melanie Klein*. New York: Totem Books, 1998.

Jacobs, Katrien, Marije Janssen, and Matteo Pasquinelli, eds. *C'Lick Me: A Netporn Studies Reader*. Amsterdam: Institute of Network Cultures, 2007. http://www.networkcultures.org/_uploads/24.pdf.

Jeffreys, Sheila. *The Idea of Prostitution*. North Melbourne: Spinifex, 1997.

Jensen, Robert. "Blow Bangs and Cluster Bombs: The Cruelty of Men and Americans." In *Not for Sale: Feminists Resisting Prostitution and Pornography*, ed. Christine Stark and Rebecca Whisnant, 28–37. North Melbourne: Spinifex, 2004.

–. *Getting Off: Pornography and the End of Masculinity*. Cambridge, MA: South End, 2007.

Jones, Amelia. *Seeing Differently: A History and Theory of Identification*. Oxford: Routledge, 2012.

Kim, Chong. "Nobody's Concubine." In *Not for Sale: Feminists Resisting Prostitution and Pornography*, ed. Christine Stark and Rebecca Whisnant, 102–5. North Melbourne: Spinifex, 2004.

Kipnis, Laura. "(Male) Desire and (Female) Disgust: Reading *Hustler*." In *Cultural Studies*, ed. Lawrence Grossberg, Cary Nelson, and Paula Treichler, 373–91. New York: Routledge, 1992.

Lacombe, Dany. *Blue Politics: Pornography and the Law in the Age of Feminism*. Toronto: University of Toronto Press, 1994. https://doi.org/10.3138/9781442671478.

Laub, Dori. "Truth and Testimony: The Process and the Struggle." In *Trauma: Explorations in Memory*, ed. Cathy Caruth, 61–75. Baltimore, MD: Johns Hopkins University Press, 1995.

Lee, Taylor. "In and Out: A Survivor's Memoir of Stripping." In *Not for Sale: Feminists Resisting Prostitution and Pornography*, ed. Christine Stark and Rebecca Whisnant, 56–63. North Melbourne: Spinifex, 2004.

Lewis, Gail. "Not by Criticality Alone." *Feminist Theory* 15, 1 (2014): 31–38. https://doi.org/10.1177/1464700113513084.

Lichtman, Chelsey. "Deeply Lez: Allyson Mitchell." Interview. *Trade* 5 (2004): 21–23.

Lighthouse Teenies. lighthouseteenseries.com.

Loveless, Natalie. "Practice in the Flesh of Theory: Art, Research, and the Fine Arts PhD." *Canadian Journal of Communication* 37, 1 (2012): 93–108. https://doi.org/10.22230/cjc.2012v37n1a2531.

MacKinnon, Catharine. *Are Women Human? And Other International Dialogues*. Cambridge, MA: Belknap, 2006.

–. "Feminism, Marxism, Method, and the State: An Agenda for Theory." 1982. In *Feminist Social Thought: A Reader*, ed. Diana Tietjens Meyers, 64–91. New York: Routledge, 1997.

–. *Feminism Unmodified: Discourses on Life and Law*. Cambridge, MA: Harvard University Press, 1987.

–. "Gender – The Future." *Constellations* 17, 4 (2010): 504–11. https://doi.org/10.1111/j.1467-8675.2010.00610.x.

–. *Only Words*. Cambridge, MA: Harvard University Press, 1993.

–. *Toward a Feminist Theory of the State*. Cambridge, MA: Harvard University Press, 1989.

–. *Women's Lives, Men's Laws*. Cambridge, MA: Belknap, 2005.

Maggie's: The Toronto Sex Workers Action Project. "Who We Are." 2011. http://maggiestoronto.ca/about.

Marcus, Sharon. "Fighting Bodies, Fighting Words: A Theory and Politics of Rape Prevention." In *Feminists Theorize the Political*, ed. Judith Butler and Joan W. Scott, 385–403. New York: Routledge, 1992.

Marcuse, Herbert. *Eros and Civilization: A Philosophical Inquiry into Freud*. 1955. Reprint, Boston: Beacon, 1966.

Mardorossian, Carine M. "Towards a New Feminist Theory of Rape." *Signs: Journal of Women in Culture and Society* 27, 3 (2002): 743–75. https://doi.org/10.1086/337938.

McNair, Brian. *Striptease Culture: Sex, Media and the Democratization of Desire*. New York: Routledge, 2002. https://doi.org/10.4324/9780203469378.

McNay, Lois. "Feminism and Post-identity Politics: The Problem of Agency." *Constellations* 17, 4 (2010): 512–25. https://doi.org/10.1111/j.1467-8675.2010.00611.x.

Millar, Thomas Macaulay. "Toward a Performance Model of Sex." In *Yes Means Yes: Visions of Female Sexual Power and a World without Rape*, ed. Jaclyn Friedman and Jessica Valenti, 29–41. Berkeley, CA: Seal, 2008.

Miriam, Kathy. "Toward a Phenomenology of Sex-Right: Reviving Radical Feminist Theory of Compulsory Heterosexuality." *Hypatia* 22, 1 (2007): 210–28. https://doi.org/10.1111/j.1527-2001.2007.tb01157.x.

Mitchell, Juliet. "Trauma, Recognition and the Place of Language." *Diacritics* 28, 4 (1998): 121–33. https://doi.org/10.1353/dia.1998.0035.

Monet, Veronica. "No Girls Allowed at the Mustang Ranch." In *Whores and Other Feminists*, ed. Jill Nagle, 167–69. New York: Routledge, 1997.

Moon, Katharine. *Sex among Allies: Military Prostitution in U.S.-Korea Relations*. New York: Columbia University Press, 1997.

Morgan, Robin. *Going Too Far: The Personal Chronicle of a Feminist*. New York: Vintage Books, 1978.

Mowlabocus, Sharif. "Porn 2.0? Technology, Social Practice, and the New Online Porn Industry." In *Porn.com: Making Sense of Online Pornography*, ed. Feona Attwood, 69–87. New York: Peter Lang, 2010.

Munt, Sally. *Queer Attachments: The Cultural Politics of Shame*. Surrey, BC: Ashgate, 2008.

Nagle, Jill. "First Ladies of Feminist Porn: A Conversation with Candida Royalle and Debi Sundahl." In *Whores and Other Feminists*, ed. Jill Nagle, 156–66. New York: Routledge, 1997.

–. "Introduction." In *Whores and Other Feminists*, ed. Jill Nagle, 1–15. New York: Routledge, 1997.

–, ed. *Whores and Other Feminists*. New York: Routledge, 1997.

Nietzsche, Friedrich. *On the Genealogy of Morality: A Polemic*. 1887. Trans. Carol Diethe. Ed. Keith Ansell-Pearson. New York: Cambridge University Press, 1997.

Paasonen, Susanna. *Carnal Resonance: Affect and Online Pornography*. Cambridge, MA: MIT Press, 2011. https://doi.org/10.7551/mitpress/9780262016315.001.0001.

–. "Disturbing, Fleshy Texts: Close Looking at Pornography." In *Working with Affect in Feminist Readings: Disturbing Differences*, ed. Marianne Liljeström and Susanna Paasonen, 58–71. Oxford: Routledge, 2010.

–. "Strange Bedfellows: Pornography, Affect and Feminist Reading." *Feminist Theory* 8, 1 (2007): 43–57. https://doi.org/10.1177/1464700107074195.

Paglia, Camille. *Sex, Art, and American Culture: Essays*. New York: Vintage Books, 1992.

Pateman, Carole. "The Fraternal Social Contract." In *Contemporary Political Philosophy: An Anthology*, 2nd ed., ed. Robert E. Goodin and Philip Pettit, 73–87. Oxford: Blackwell Publishers Ltd., 2006 (1980).

Pendleton, Eva. "Love for Sale: Queering Heterosexuality." In *Whores and Other Feminists*, ed. Jill Nagle, 73–82. New York: Routledge, 1997.

"Penetration." In *Webster's New World College Dictionary*. 2014. http://www.yourdictionary.com/penetration.

Petro, Melissa. "Selling Sex: Women's Participation in the Sex Industry." In *Sex Work Matters: Exploring Money, Power and Intimacy in the Sex Industry*, ed. Melissa Hope Ditmore, Antonia Levy, and Alys Willman, 155–70. London: Zed Books, 2010.

Philadelphoff-Puren, Nina. "The Mark of Refusal: Sexual Violence and the Politics of Recontextualization." *Feminist Theory* 5, 3 (2004): 243–56. https://doi.org/10.1177/1464700104046975.

Probyn, Elspeth. *Blush: Faces of Shame*. Minneapolis: University of Minnesota Press, 2005.

Queen, Carol. "Sex Radical Politics, Sex-Positive Feminist Thought, and Whore Stigma." In *Whores and Other Feminists*, ed. Jill Nagle, 125–35. New York: Routledge, 1997.

Razack, Sherene. "Race, Space, and Prostitution: The Making of the Bourgeois Subject." *Canadian Journal of Women and the Law* 10, 2 (1998): 338–76.

Rich, Adrienne. "Compulsory Heterosexuality and Lesbian Existence." 1980. In *Blood, Bread, and Poetry: Selected Prose, 1979–1985*, 23–75. New York: W.W. Norton, 1986.

Roiphe, Katie. "Date Rape's Other Victim." *New York Times*, June 13, 1993. http://www.nytimes.com/1993/06/13/magazine/date-rape-s-other-victim.html.

Rose, Jacqueline. *Sexuality in the Field of Vision*. 1986. Reprint, New York: Verso, 2005.

Rosenberg, Sharon. "Intersecting Memories: Bearing Witness to the 1989 Massacre of Women in Montreal." *Hypatia* 11, 4 (1996): 119–29. https://doi.org/10.1111/j.1527-2001.1996.tb01039.x.

–. "Neither Forgotten nor Fully Remembered: Tracing an Ambivalent Public Memory on the 10th Anniversary of the Montreal Massacre." *Feminist Theory* 4, 1 (2003): 5–27. https://doi.org/10.1177/1464700103004001001.

Rubin, Gayle. "Thinking Sex." In *Pleasure and Danger: Exploring Female Sexuality*, ed. Carole S. Vance, 267–319. Boston: Routledge and Keegan Paul, 1984.

Salecl, Renata. "Society of Choice." *Differences: A Journal of Feminist Cultural Studies* 20, 1 (2009): 157–80. https://doi.org/10.1215/10407391-2008-020.

Sartre, Jean-Paul. *No Exit: And Three Other Plays*. 1946. Reprint, New York: Vintage International, 1989.

Scoular, Jane. "The 'Subject' of Prostitution: Interpreting the Discursive, Symbolic and Material Position of Sex/Work in Feminist Theory." *Feminist Theory* 5, 3 (2004): 343–55. https://doi.org/10.1177/1464700104046983.

Sedgwick, Eve Kosofsky. *Touching Feeling: Affect, Pedagogy, Performativity*. Durham, NC: Duke University Press, 2003.

Segal, Lynne. "Does Pornography Cause Violence? The Search for Evidence." In *Dirty Looks: Women, Pornography, Power*, ed. Pamela Church Gibson and Roma Gibson, 5–21. London: British Film Institute, 1993.

–. "Sweet Sorrows, Painful Pleasures: Pornography and the Perils of Heterosexual Desire." In *Sex Exposed: Sexuality and the Pornography Debate*, ed. Lynne Segal and Mary McIntosh, 65–91. New Brunswick, NJ: Rutgers University Press, 1993.

Serisier, Tayna. "Who Was Andrea? Writing Oneself as a Feminist Icon." *Women: A Cultural Review* 24, 1 (2013): 26–44. https://doi.org/10.1080/09574042.2012.751794.

Sheiner, Marcy. "Odyssey of a Feminist Pornographer." In *Whores and Other Feminists*, ed. Jill Nagle, 36–43. New York: Routledge, 1997.

Simonton, Ann, and Carol Smith. "Who Are Women in Pornography? A Conversation." In *Not for Sale: Feminists Resisting Prostitution and Pornography*, ed. Christine Stark and Rebecca Whisnant, 352–61. North Melbourne: Spinifex, 2004.

Stacey, Jackie. "Wishing Away Ambivalence." *Feminist Theory* 15, 1 (2014): 39–49. https://doi.org/10.1177/1464700113513083.

Stark, Christine. "Girls to Boyz: Sex Radical Women Promoting Pornography and Prostitution." In *Not for Sale: Feminists Resisting Prostitution and Pornography*, ed. Christine Stark and Rebecca Whisnant, 278–92. North Melbourne: Spinifex, 2004.

Stark, Christine, and Rebecca Whisnant, eds. *Not for Sale: Feminists Resisting Prostitution and Pornography*. North Melbourne: Spinifex, 2004.

Stein, Ruth. *Psychoanalytic Theories of Affect*. New York: Praeger, 1991.

Tiersma, Peter M. "The Language of Consent in Rape Law." In *The Language of Sexual Crime*, ed. Janet Cotterill, 83–103. New York: Palgrave Macmillan, 2007. https://doi.org/10.1057/9780230592780_5.

Tomlinson, Barbara. *Feminism and Affect at the Scene of the Argument: Beyond the Trope of the Angry Feminist*. Philadelphia: Temple University Press, 2010.

van der Meulen, Emily. "Canadian and International Policies on Prostitution: Labour Legitimacy, Social Change, and Decriminalization." In *Public Policy for Women: The State, Income Security, and Labour Market Issues*, ed. Marjorie Griffin Cohen and Jane Pulkingham, 332–52. Toronto: University of Toronto Press, 2009.

van Dijck, José. "Users Like You? Theorizing Agency in User-Generated Content." *Media, Culture and Society* 31, 1 (2009): 41–58. https://doi.org/10.1177/0163443708098245.

Vogels, Josey. "Vampire Mania: It's All about Sex." *Toronto Metro*, November 17, 2009.

Waskul, Dennis. *Net.seXXX: Readings on Sex, Pornography and the Internet*. New York: Peter Lang, 2004.

Whisnant, Rebecca, and Christine Stark. "Introduction." In *Not for Sale: Feminists Resisting Prostitution and Pornography*, ed. Christine Stark and Rebecca Whisnant, xi–xvii. North Melbourne: Spinifex, 2004.

Wicke, Jennifer. "Through a Gaze Darkly: Pornography's Academic Market." In *Dirty Looks: Women, Pornography, Power*, ed. Pamela Church Gibson and Roma Gibson, 62–80. London: British Film Institute, 1993.

Wiegman, Robyn. *Object Lessons*. Durham, NC: Duke University Press, 2012.

–. "The Times We're In: Queer Feminist Criticism and the Reparative 'Turn.'" *Feminist Theory* 15, 1 (2014): 4–25. https://doi.org/10.1177/1464700113513081a.

Woods, Alastair. "Feeling the Political: Trauma and Affect in Contemporary Liberal Capitalism." Undergraduate thesis, York University, 2011.

Žižek, Slavoj. *The Sublime Object of Ideology*. New York: Verso, 1989.

Index

affective attachments to theory, 10–13, 79–80, 82, 103–5; ambivalent attachments, 20, 84, 106–8; difficulty in shifting, 105–6; passionate attachments, 5–6, 10, 13, 92, 98, 107
affects, 56–57, 111*n*27; role in repressed memories, 86–87. *See also* affective attachments to theory; emotions
Ahmed, Sara, 12, 42, 46, 50, 52, 56–57, 58, 59, 99
Albury, Kate, 94, 132*n*61
Alexander, Priscilla, 63
anti-pornography feminism, 18–19, 52–54, 79
attachment. *See* affective attachments to theory

BDSM, 68, 111*n*44, 125*n*35, 126*n*54
Bell, Shannon, 93–94, 114*n*67, 117*n*44, 126*n*56, 131*n*51
Berlant, Lauren, 104, 134*n*3, 134*n*4, 134*n*6
Bernstein, Elizabeth, 53–54
Bersani, Leo: Ancient Greek views on male homosexuality, 24–25; sex as unredeemable, 117*n*49, 118*n*50; sexual pleasure, 33–34, 35–36, 117*n*48
Bill C-36 (Canada, 2014), 62, 122*n*6
Bill C-49 (Canada, 1992), 49–50
Bonnycastle, Kevin, 49–50, 57, 120*n*32
Bright, Susie, 63
Britzman, Deborah, 11, 13, 94, 133*n*76
Brock, Deborah, 126*n*56
Brown, Laura S., 87, 130*n*22
Brown, Wendy, 57, 96–97
Brownmiller, Susan, 15, 41, 118*n*1
butch-femme relations, 16, 36–37, 92
Butler, Judith: the interpellative hail, 11, 106; melancholia, 91; sexual differences, 34–35; social agents as objects, 27–28, 81; subject formation, 8, 11, 103–4, 106

Cahill, Ann J., 41, 45–48, 85, 118*n*1, 119*n*14, 119*n*23
Canada. *An Act to amend the Criminal Code (sexual assault)*, 1992. *See* Bill C-49 (Canada, 1992)

148 *Index*

Canada. *Protection of Communities and Exploited Persons Act*, 2014. *See* Bill C-36 (Canada, 2014)
Caruth, Cathy, 85
cathexis, 10, 79
celibacy movement, 70
commodification: of sex, 19, 70–71, 80, 122*n*6, 126*n*47; of women, 61, 125*n*45. *See also* sex work
consciousness-raising, 52
consensual sex, 70–71; consent vs consensus, 57–59, 60; emotional aspects, 17, 55–56, 57, 58–59; nonconsensual sex vs, 43–47, 53–56. *See also* consent
consent, 120*n*32; consensus vs, 57–59, 60; unequal power relations and, 57–58. *See also* consensual sex
continuum of heterosexual violence, 14–15, 17, 41–42, 43–47, 59
Cowie, Elizabeth, 73, 74, 81–82, 93, 127*n*71
Criminal Code of Canada: revisions, 49–50
Crow, Barbara A., 110*n*3
cultural representations, 23–26
Cvetkovich, Ann: femme sexuality, 36–37, 92; overlap of affect, emotion and feeling, 12, 111*n*27; reparative viewpoint, 92, 93, 110*n*4; touch as trauma, 33–34; views on affect, 54–55, 121*n*48

date rape, 47–49, 51, 96, 113*n*47, 119*n*25
desire, 19, 29–30, 62, 72–76, 93, 127*n*69; related to powerlessness, 36–37; sex-positive viewpoints, 44, 57, 92; sex work and, 74–75, 81–82, 127*n*68; views of Andrea Dworkin on, 29, 30–32, 37, 117*n*34
Dines, Gail, 18, 113*n*54

discourse, 7, 134*n*11; as element of lived reality, 26–27. *See also* feminist sex wars; paranoid position; patriarchal discourse; radical feminism; reparative position; sex-positive feminism
Dworkin, Andrea: affective labour of her writings, 33, 35–36; inflammatory writing style, 22, 39, 86; paranoid position, 88–92, 97; reasons work frequently dismissed, 16, 22–23, 29–32, 38–40; *ressentiment*, 97; views on gendered anatomy, 28, 94, 116*n*27, 116*n*28; views on heterosexual desire, 29, 30–32, 37, 117*n*34; views on heterosexual intercourse, 14–15, 16, 21–29, 23, 37–40, 88, 115*n*5, 117*n*34, 124*n*27; views on pornography, 17; views on romantic love, 88; views on sexual assault, 14–15, 41, 86, 119*n*14; works, 65, 115*n*4, 124*n*23
Dymock, Alex, 126*n*54

either-or theory of sexual assault, 17, 41, 47–51, 59–60
emotions, 111*n*27; interpretive functions of, 42–43, 46–47, 50–51, 55; reactions to pornography, 52–53, 76–80; role in feminist arguments, 52–57. *See also* affective attachments to theory; affects; desire; shame
empowerment: female agency and either/or theory of assault, 48–49, 59–60
ethical ambiguity, 43–44, 45–46, 51, 59

false consciousness: Dworkin's views on heterosexual desire and, 31–32
fantasy, 27*n*71, 73–76, 81–82, 93; BDSM community, 125*n*35
feelings. *See* affects; emotions

Felman, Shoshana, 10, 86, 109*n*2
female phallus, 93–94, 117*n*44
feminist frameworks, 4, 6, 109*n*1; divisions between feminisms, 65–66, 124*n*24; effects on emotions, thoughts and bodies, 42, 46, 50–51, 111*n*26; reconciliation of, 9, 109*n*1, 109*n*3. *See also* affective attachments to theory; paranoid position; poststructural feminism; radical feminism; reparative position; sex-positive feminism
feminist identity: divisions between feminisms, 65–66, 124*n*24; Dworkin's views on heterosexual desire and, 32; feminist sex wars, 4, 5, 6, 13–14, 63, 103
feminist knowledges, 5, 67, 124*n*28. *See also* feminist frameworks
Feminist Porn Awards, 61–62, 63
feminist sex wars, 4, 5, 6, 13–14, 63, 103
femme sexuality, 16, 36–37, 92
Fernflores, Rachel, 22, 115*n*4
the field imaginary, 104
Foucault, Michel, 7–8, 39, 120*n*33, 121*n*48; repressive hypothesis of sexuality, 19, 62–65, 67, 72, 81, 123*n*14, 123*n*17

Gavey, Nicola, 43–44, 45, 51, 119*n*10, 119*n*25
gendered violence: reparative readings of, 99–101; role of radical feminism in witnessing, 20, 84, 85–88, 90–91, 96, 100. *See also* intercourse-as-violation discourse; sexual assault

Halberstam, Judith/Jack, 99
Hall, Stuart, 26, 27
Hard Love and How to Fuck in High Heels (film), 94

have/hold discourse, 44
Hemmings, Clare, 107, 109*n*1
heterosexual desire. *See* desire
heterosexual intercourse: penetration, 16, 23–25, 33, 34, 36, 37, 92, 113*n*56; sexual pleasure and powerlessness, 24, 33–37. *See also* intercourse-as-violation discourse
heterosexual pornography. *See* pornography
hope, 94–95, 101, 133*n*76
humiliation theory, 90

identification, 13, 27–28, 76–79, 82, 128*n*79, 128*n*80. *See also* affective attachments to theory
ideology, 6–7, 31–32; sexuality and, 35–36
insidious rape trauma, 87–88, 100
intercourse. *See* heterosexual intercourse; intercourse-as-violation discourse
intercourse-as-violation discourse, 21–22; critiques of, 22–29, 37–40; desire and, 29–32; as investigation of political meaning, 23–29; penetration, 16, 23–25, 33, 34, 36, 37, 92, 113*n*56; production of gendered actors and, 22–23, 27–29, 33–35; related to sexual assault, 45–46. *See also* gendered violence; sexual assault

James, E.L., 126*n*54
Jeffreys, Sheila, 18
Jensen, Robert, 52, 115*n*10
Jones, Amelia, 77, 128*n*79

Kipnis, Laura, 77
Klein, Bonnie Sherr, 53
Klein, Melanie, 4, 83–84, 107–8, 129*n*2

Lewis, Gail, 133*n*75, 135*n*14
Love, Heather, 98
Loveless, Natalie, 10

MacKinnon, Catharine, 88, 89–90, 118*n*50; views on consent, 57; views on pornography, 17–18, 52, 61, 118*n*50, 129*n*88; views on sex work, 18, 61, 121*n*40; views on sexual assault, 14, 15, 41–42, 118*n*50, 119*n*14; views on sexuality, 14, 88, 110*n*5, 112*n*37, 130*n*26
Maggie's: The Toronto Sex Workers Action Project, 62, 63
male homosexuality, 15, 23–24, 25
manic-reparation, 20, 84–85, 95–96, 98–99, 100, 132*n*68
Marcus, Sharon, 50, 120*n*33, 126*n*49
Marcuse, Herbert, 123*n*14
Mardorossian, Carine M., 120*n*33
McNair, Brian, 132*n*66
McNay, Lois, 100–1
melancholia, 91, 99
Millar, Thomas Macaulay, 70, 80–81, 93, 125*n*44
Millett, Kate, 18, 75
Miriam, Kathy, 110*n*5
Mitchell, Allyson, 109*n*3
Mitchell, Juliet, 85
modernist discourses, 6–7, 31–32. *See also* radical feminism
Monet, Veronica, 63
Mowlabocus, Sharif, 68, 114*n*61, 125*n*34
Munt, Sally, 78, 79

Nagle, Jill, 80
naming of sexual encounters: difficulties in, 43–47, 51–52, 59–60
Not a Love Story (film), 53
Not for Sale (anthology), 52–53, 114*n*59, 124*n*24

Paasonen, Susanna, 12, 53, 54, 76, 100
Paglia, Camille, 16, 47–49, 60, 96, 113*n*46, 113*n*48, 119*n*19
paranoid position, 129*n*2; ambivalence and, 107–8; Melanie Klein, 83–84; radical feminism, 20, 84, 88–92, 96–97, 99, 100, 131*n*46; as strong theory, 90–91, 131*n*40
paranoid-schizoid position. *See* paranoid position
patriarchal discourse, 4, 15, 17, 61, 66–67, 75, 89, 119*n*10; sexual assault, 41–42, 44–45
Pendleton, Eva, 69–70, 71; manic reparation, 95–96
penetration, 16, 23–25, 33, 34, 36, 37, 92, 113*n*56
permissive sex discourse, 44, 119*n*10
Petro, Melissa, 114*n*65
phallic entitlement, 127*n*65; female phallus, 93–94, 117*n*44
phallocentrism, 36, 118*n*49
popular culture, 23–26
pornography, 67; affective aspects, 52–53, 76–80; dominance and submission in, 67–68, 115*n*10; fantasy and, 73–76, 93, 125*n*35; popular tropes, 25, 73–74, 93, 127*n*65; privileging of male heterosexual viewpoints, 67–69; reparative readings of, 94; views of radical feminists on, 17–18, 52, 61, 78, 118*n*50, 129*n*88; views of sex-positive feminists on, 18–19, 61–66, 77, 82; websites, 68–69, 114*n*61, 115*n*15, 124*n*31, 125*n*34. *See also* anti-pornography feminism
poststructural feminism, 6, 111*n*26; conceptualization of power, 7–8, 19, 111*n*34; identity politics and, 8–9
poststructural theory, 4, 6, 7

power, 7–8; consent and, 57–58; poststructuralist views on, 7–8, 19, 111*n*34; radical feminist views on, 8, 30, 104, 111*n*34. *See also* empowerment; penetration; powerlessness
powerlessness, 35–37, 118*n*51; butch-femme relations and, 16; sexual pleasure and, 24, 33–37
Probyn, Elspeth, 79
prostitution. *See* sex work

Queen, Carol, 81
queer feminism, 6

race (concept), 27
radical feminism, 109*n*3, 110*n*5; conservative Christianity and, 63, 65; feminist sex wars and, 4, 13–16, 103; focus on narratives of exclusion, 96–97, 99, 100; identity politics and, 8, 9; male radical feminists, 128*n*84; paranoid position, 20, 84, 88–92, 96–97, 99, 100, 131*n*46; reinvention of sex and, 66–67, 117*n*49, 118*n*50; role in witnessing gendered violence, 20, 84, 85–88, 90–91, 96, 100; as sex-negative, 4, 124*n*24; unfair characterizations of, 6; use of affective argument, 52–53, 54; views on pornography, 17–18, 61, 78; views on power, 8, 30, 104, 111*n*34; views on sex work, 18, 61, 63, 65, 78. *See also* Dworkin, Andrea; intercourse-as-violation discourse; MacKinnon, Catharine; patriarchal discourse
rape: date rape, 47–49, 51, 96, 113*n*47, 119*n*25; insidious rape trauma, 87–88, 100. *See also* sexual assault
Razack, Sheren, 126*n*53

reparative-depressive position. *See* reparative position
reparative position, 91, 129*n*2; ambivalence and, 107–8; as healing, 100–1; Melanie Klein, 83–84; manic-reparation, 95–96, 98–99, 100; sex-positive feminism and, 92–96, 98–99
representation, 8–9
repression of sexuality: alternatives to resistance, 80–81; repressive hypothesis, 19, 62–65, 67, 72, 81, 123*n*14, 123*n*17; resistance as transgression, 63–65, 71–72; resistance to patriarchy, 66–67
ressentiment, 97
Roiphe, Katie, 113*n*47, 113*n*48
Rose, Jacqueline, 73, 106–7, 134*n*11
Rosenberg, Sharon, 14, 85, 87
Royalle, Candida, 63
Rubin, Gayle, 63, 126*n*56

Salecl, Renata, 128*n*75
Scoular, Jane, 70
Sedgwick, Eve Kosofsky, 54, 56; analysis of paranoid positions, 83–84, 88–91, 132*n*68; knowledge as performative, 83–84; reparation, 94, 107, 132*n*51
Segal, Lynne, 73, 74, 93, 127*n*65
Serisier, Tayna, 22, 115*n*4
sex: as collaborative performance, 80–81; commodification of, 19, 70–71, 80, 122*n*6, 126*n*47; ethical ambiguity and, 43–44, 45–46, 51, 59; reinvention of, 66–67, 117*n*49, 118*n*50. *See also* consensual sex; heterosexual intercourse; sexual assault; sexual pleasure
sex-positive feminism, 4, 15–16; feminist sex wars, 4, 13–15; manic-reparation, 20, 84–85, 95–96, 98–99,

100, 132*n*68; reparative position, 84–85; tendency toward omnipotence, 98, 133*n*75, 133*n*76; use of affective argument, 53–54; views on pornography and sex work, 18–19, 61–66, 77–78, 82; views on sexual assault, 112*n*45

sex work, 71, 113*n*56, 114*n*59, 114*n*65; affective aspects, 52, 53–54, 71, 76; as challenge to heteronormativity, 69–70, 71, 95–96; questioning of transgressive nature, 72, 126*n*56; as reproducing heteronormativity, 70–71; role of fantasy in, 74–76; romanticization of, 126*n*53; worker paradigm, 123*n*13

sexual assault: as constituted in the Criminal Code of Canada, 49–50, 120*n*32; as continuum of heterosexual violence, 14–15, 17, 41–42, 43–47, 59; date rape, 47–49, 51, 96, 113*n*47, 119*n*25; as distinct from sex (either-or), 17, 41, 47–51, 59–60; feminization of women as subjects of fear, 50–51; insidious rape trauma, 87–88, 100; non-consent and, 43–47, 55–56; perception of assault related to emotions, 17, 42–43, 50–51; role of sexuality as an object of exchange in, 70–71

sexual drive discourse, 44

sexual pleasure: powerlessness and, 24, 33–37; psychic shattering and, 33–34, 35; in sex-positive argumentation, 16, 54, 63, 65–66

sexuality. *See* desire; repression of sexuality; sex; sexual pleasure

shame, 19–20, 62, 78–80, 82

Sheiner, Marcy, 53

socialist feminism, 4, 111*n*34

Stacey, Jackie, 107

Stark, Christine, 112*n*44, 124*n*24

Stein, Ruth, 42, 85–86

theory: psychic significance of, 11–13. *See also* affective attachments to theory; feminist frameworks

Tiersma, Peter M., 55, 121*n*50

touch, 33–34, 36, 51

trauma, 130*n*22; radical feminism and, 85–88

triumphalism, 133*n*75

vampires in popular culture, 25–26

warfare: sexualization of, 24

Whisnant, Rebecca, 124*n*24

Wicke, Jennifer, 22

Wiegman, Robyn, 10, 14, 99, 107, 134*n*5, 135*n*14

women: commodification of, 61, 125*n*45